HOT TOPICS

Hands-on activities • Investigations • Model-making ... and much more!

Olympics

ages 5-11 for all primary years

Peter Riley

Author
Peter Riley

Development Editor
Kate Pedlar

Editor
Roanne Charles

Project Editor
Fabia Lewis

Cover and inside illustrations
Laszlo Veres/Beehive Illustration

Photocopiable page illustrations
Colin Elgie

Back cover photograph
Peter Rowe

Model-making
Linda Jones

Polaroid photos
Linda Jones

Series Designer
Helen Taylor

Cover concept/designer
Catherine Perera

This book is dedicated to Sam Tasker.

British Library Cataloguing-in-Publication Data
A catalogue record for this book is available from the British Library.

ISBN 978-0439-94573-8

Designed using Adobe InDesign

Published by Scholastic Ltd
Book End
Range Road
Witney
Oxfordshire OX29 0YD

www.scholastic.co.uk

Printed by Bell & Bain, Glasgow

5 6 7 8 9 1 2 3 4 5 6 7

Contents

PHOTOGRAPH © ALLISON PARRY

Introduction

The *Hot Topics* series explores topics that can be taught across the curriculum. Each book divides its topic into a number of themes that can be worked through progressively to build up a firm foundation of knowledge and provide opportunities for developing a wide range of skills. Each theme provides background information and three lesson plans, for ages 5–7, 7–9 and 9–11. Each lesson plan looks at a different aspect of the theme and varies in complexity, from a simple approach with younger children, to a more complex approach with older children. There are also photocopiable sheets to support the lessons in each theme.

BACKGROUND INFORMATION

Each theme starts by providing information to support you in teaching the lesson. You may share it with the children as part of your own lesson plan or use it to help answer some of the children's questions as they arise. Information is given about the photocopiable sheets as well as the answers to any questions which have been set. This section also provides a brief overview of all three lessons, to help you select content for your own sessions.

The lessons

A detailed structure is provided for lessons aimed at children who are in the 7–9 age range. Less detailed plans, covering all the essentials, are given for the lessons aimed at the other two age ranges, so covering the entire primary age range.

Detailed lesson plans

The detailed lesson plans have the following format:

Objectives

The content of all lesson plans is focused on specific objectives related to the study of the Olympics.

Subject references

All lesson plans show how they relate to specific curriculum-related objectives. These objectives are based on statements in the National Curriculum for England. They may be used as they are, or regarded as an illustration of the statements that may be addressed, helping you to find others which you consider more appropriate for your needs.

Resources and preparation

This section lists everything you will need to deliver the lesson, including any photocopiables provided in this book. Preparation describes anything that needs to be done in advance of the lesson, for example making a model Greek temple. As part of the preparation, you should consult your school's policies on all practical work so that you can select activities for which you are confident to take responsibility.

Starter
A starter is only provided in the more detailed lesson plans for ages 7–9. It provides an introduction to the lesson, helping the children to focus on the topic and generate interest.

What to do
This section sets out, point by point, the sequence of activities in the main part of the lesson. It may include activities for you to do, but concentrates mainly on the children's work.

Differentiation
Differentiation is only provided in the more detailed lesson plans for ages 7–9. Suggestions are given for developing strategies for support and extension activities.

Assessment
This section is only provided in the lesson plans for the 7–9 age range. It suggests ways to assess children, either through the product of their work or through looking at how they performed in an activity.

Plenary
A Plenary is only provided in the lesson plans for the 7–9 age range. It shows how children can review their own work and assess their progress in learning about the Olympics. It is not related to other lessons, but if you are planning a sequence of lessons, you may also like to use it to generate interest, in future studies of the Olympics.

Outcomes
These are only provided in the lesson plans for the 7–9 age range. They relate to the general objectives. You may wish to add more specific outcomes related to the context in which you use the lesson.

Extension
This section is found in the lesson plans for 5–7 and 9–11 year olds. It allows you to take the initial content of the lesson further.

Flexibility and extra differentiation
As the lessons in each topic are clustered around a particular theme, you may wish to add parts of one lesson to parts of another. For example in Theme 1, 'The Ancient Greeks' you may choose to add parts of Lessons 1 and 2 about Ancient Greek pottery and statues, to Lesson 3, which deals with maps of Ancient Greece.

In the lesson plans for 7–9 year olds, differentiation is addressed directly, with its own section. In lessons for the other age groups, differentiation is addressed by providing ideas for extension work. The themes, however, are arranged so that you may also pick activities from the different age groups to provide differentiation. For example, in a lesson for ages 5–7 you may wish to add activities from the lesson for 7–9 year olds, in the same theme.

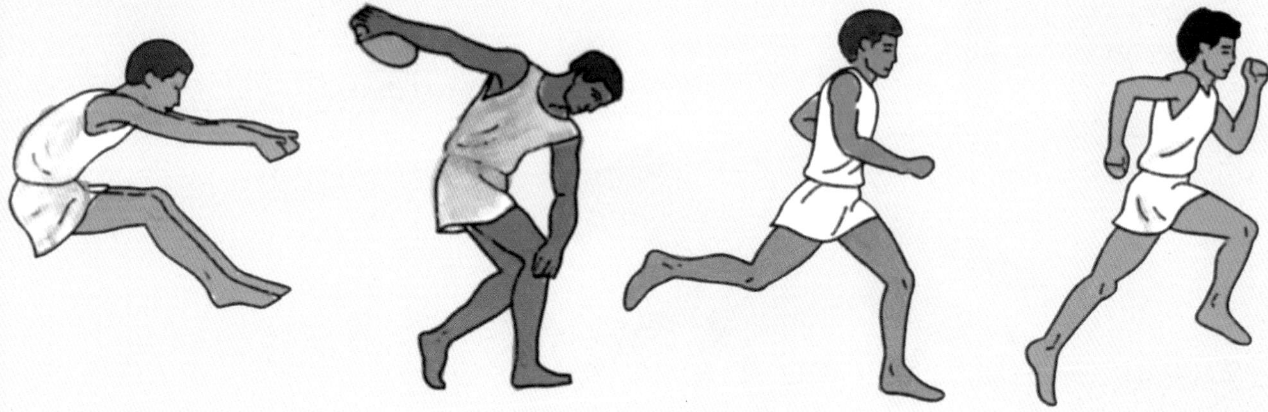

Planning a project

You may like to use the topic for a class or school project culminating in an Olympics Day. This will need considerable preparation, but the result could be a very memorable event! This section provides some suggestions for activities leading up to the day and for a programme of events.

The suggested activities in the tables of this section, are featured in or based on the lesson plans shown in the third column. Read through each lesson plan to work out how the activity can fit into the context of your Olympics Day.

Times are given for guidance only. Depending on your circumstances, you may want to lengthen or shorten any activity.

Olympics Day Ages 5–7

Preparation

- If appropriate, send a letter home asking parents or carers to help make Ancient Greek costumes (see pictures on pages 13 and 14 for guidance). If you feel that some children are unlikely to bring a costume, collect items that they could wear. They will also need their PE kits, for the afternoon events.
- A feature of the day could be an Ancient Greek meal, so mention this in the letter home. Suitable foods are listed in the Background section on page 16. Drinks could be grape juice and still water.
- As the children proceed through the topics, the classroom can be decorated with Greek 'pottery', model houses, temples, chariots, medals and mascots. (You may like to leave making olive-branch wreaths until the day.)
- The children can also practise sporting skills for the afternoon competition. If it is a wet afternoon, the children could try the pentathlon board game (Theme 6 lesson 2) or make up games for indoor Olympics (Theme 7 lesson 2).

	Ages 5–7	Activity	Lesson plan	Pages
MORNING	10 minutes	Procession of costumes accompanied by the music from the 'Olympic Song'	Champions Theme 9, Lesson 1	73/77
MORNING	30–40 minutes	Making a Greek home	Life in Ancient Greece Theme 2, Lesson 1	17/21
MORNING	30–40 minutes	Olympic sports	The ancient games Theme 4, Lesson 1	33/37
MORNING	15 minutes	Song rehearsal	Champions Theme 9, Lesson 1	73/77
MORNING	30 minutes	Chariot racing (older children could make the chariots beforehand)	The ancient games Theme 4, Lesson 2	34/ 37–9
AFTERNOON	10 minutes	Procession to the sports field, with or without music	Champions Theme 9, Lesson 1	73/77
AFTERNOON	5–10 minutes	Opening ceremony	Ancient to modern Theme 5, Lessons 1 and 3	41, 44/ 45
AFTERNOON	60–90 minutes	Competitions (taking part and watching)	Going to the games Theme 3, Lesson 1	25/29
AFTERNOON	15–20 minutes	Closing ceremony: award medals/wreaths; song performance	Ancient to modern Theme 5, Lessons 1 and 3 Champions Theme 9, Lesson 1	41, 44/ 45 73/77

Olympics Day Ages 7–9

Preparation

- Make sure that you have covered all the preparation needed to carry out the lessons on the Olympics Day. If appropriate, send a letter home asking parents and carers to help make Ancient Greek costumes (see the pictures on pages 13 and 14 for guidance). If you feel that some children are unlikely to bring a costume, collect items that they could use. They will also need their PE kits for the afternoon events.
- A feature of the day could be an Ancient Greek meal, so mention this in the letter home. Suitable foods are listed in the Background section on page 16. Drinks could be grape juice and still water.
- As the children proceed through the topics, the classroom can be decorated in Greek model houses, temples, chariots and maps etc. (You may like to leave making olive-branch wreaths until the day.)
- Let the children practise sporting skills for the afternoon competition.
- If it is a wet afternoon, the children could try the pentathlon board game or the computer games at http://abc.net.au/olympics/2004/kayak.htm and http://abc.net.au/olympics/2004/skeet_shooting.htm.

Olympics Day Ages 9–11

Preparation

- If appropriate, send a letter home asking parents or carers to help make Ancient Greek costumes (see pictures on pages 13 and 14 for guidance). If you feel some children are unlikely to bring a costume, collect items that they could wear. They will also need their PE kits.
- If you plan an athlete's visit, write to him or her, in advance, with the ideas for an interview with the children.
- If it is a wet afternoon, you could organise some simple indoor games and finish with an award ceremony.

	Ages 7–9	Activity	Lesson plan	Pages
MORNING	10 minutes	Procession of costumes accompanied by the music from the 'Olympic Song'	Champions Theme 9, Lesson 1	73/77
MORNING	40 minutes	Greek pottery	The Ancient Greeks Theme 1, Lesson 1	9/13
MORNING	30 minutes	Making olive-branch wreaths	Ancient to modern Theme 5, Lesson 1	41/45
MORNING	60 minutes	Making and racing chariots	The ancient games Theme 4, Lessons 2 and 3	34–6/ 37–9
AFTERNOON	10 minutes	Procession to the sports field, with or without music	Champions Theme 9, Lesson 1	73/77
AFTERNOON	5–10 minutes	Opening ceremony	Ancient to modern Theme 5, Lessons 1 and 3	41, 44/ 45, 47
AFTERNOON	60–90 minutes	Competitions (taking part and watching)	Outdoor Olympics Theme 6, Lesson 2	50/54
AFTERNOON	15–20 minutes	Closing ceremony: award medals/wreaths; song performance	Ancient to modern Theme 5, Lessons 1 and 3 Champions Theme 9, Lesson 1	41, 44/ 45, 47/ 73, 77

	Ages 9–11	Activity	Lesson plan	Pages
MORNING	20 minutes	Making olive-branch wreaths	Ancient to modern Theme 5, Lessons 1 and 3	41, 44/ 45, 47
MORNING	40 minutes	Making and racing chariots	The ancient games Theme 4, Lessons 2 and 3	34–6/ 37
MORNING	30 minutes	Interview with sports person	Champions Theme 9, Lesson 3	76/79
MORNING	20 minutes	Making medals (for the afternoon competition)	Champions Theme 9, Lesson 2	74–5/ 78
AFTERNOON	10 minutes	Procession to the sports field, with or without music	Champions Theme 9, Lesson 1	73/77
AFTERNOON	5-10 minutes	Opening ceremony with torch relay	Ancient to modern Theme 5, Lesson 3 Outdoor Olympics Theme 6, Lesson 3	44/47 52/55
AFTERNOON	40 minutes	Competition	Outdoor Olympics Theme 6, Lessons 2 and 3	50–2/ 54–5
AFTERNOON	20 minutes	Closing ceremony: award medals/wreaths; song	Ancient to modern Theme 5, Lessons 1 and 3 Champions Theme 9, Lesson 1	41, 44/ 45, 47 73, 77

The Ancient Greeks

BACKGROUND

Greece is mountainous, so Ancient Greek settlements were fairly isolated. Settlements had their own laws and government and they often fought each other for land. Sometimes they joined forces against other countries.

Wheat, vines and olives were cultivated in the valleys. Goats were the main farm animal, although oxen were kept in order to pull ploughs. Fishing was also important.

The Ancient Greeks were skilled potters and they decorated their pots with everyday scenes, or activities related to the gods. They also made fine bronze statues and smaller terracotta figures. The Greeks enjoyed music and they played a range of instruments including the lyre (a stringed instrument) and the aulos (a wind instrument with two pipes). They also enjoyed drama, during which the actors wore large masks.

In time, settlements sprang up outside Greece, but athletes would return to take part in the Olympic Games. The first games took place in 776BC and the last in 393AD. The ancient Olympics took place 293 times.

IMAGE © VASANTDAVE/STOCKXCHNG

THE CONTENTS

Lesson 1 (Ages 5–7)
Ancient Greek pottery
The children excavate and assemble pieces of 'pottery' to find out about life in Ancient Greece.

Lesson 2 (Ages 7–9)
Statues and figures
The children look at archaeological evidence to deduce more about the Ancient Greeks.

Lesson 3 (Ages 9–11)
Ancient Greece
The children identify some of the important settlements in Ancient Greece. They plot routes travelled, from some of the distant places, in the Greek Empire, to Olympia and construct a timeline to set the Ancient Greeks and the founding of the modern Olympics in context.

Notes on photocopiables
Ancient Greek pottery (page 13)
The hydria (jar) shows a hunter wearing a large sunhat, cloak, shoes and leggings. He carries two spears and has a dog with him. Beneath him is a fisherman, using a rod and net. The amphora (large jar) shows a fishmonger poised to cut a piece of fish and, a baby on a potty, waving a rattle. The krater shows a man, holding a scroll. Beneath him is a boy rolling a hoop and carrying a tray of food. The oinchoe (jug) shows a woman playing an aulos. Children may note that the fisherman and boy are naked. This was perfectly acceptable – Olympic competitors were also naked.

Statues and figures (page 14)
1) Soldier wearing a helmet, a cuirass (armour covering his torso) and a short tunic. He is carrying a shield and spear. 2) Man wearing a tunic and sandals. 3) Woman wearing a dress called a peplos, pinned at the shoulder. 4) Farmer with a plough and two oxen. He is wearing a tunic. 5) Masked actor – the large, smiling mouth signifies that he is playing a comical character. 6) Musician playing a five-stringed lyre.

Ancient Greece (page 15)
Map 1 shows ten important settlements in Ancient Greece.

Lesson 1 Ancient Greek pottery

Resources and preparation

- Photocopy page 13 onto card and cut out the pottery (enlarge items if required). Then cut each item into several parts, depending on the children's age or ability. Bury each set of parts in a shallow dish of dry sand. Collect clean food containers such as jars, tins, bottles, plates, bowls and jugs.
- Each pair of children will need a dish of buried 'pottery', a spoon, a medium/thick paintbrush, A4 card and scissors.

What to do

- Show the children the food containers, and elicit that we use these when we store food or have a meal. Ask what usually happens to such objects when they are broken or finished with. Ask what happens to items such as pottery and wood (for example wooden spoons) when they are buried in the ground. Talk about wood rotting away, but pottery being preserved. You could go on to look at the properties of pottery (clay) to show why it is used to make strong, watertight containers.
- Tell the children that the Ancient Greeks also used pottery for storing food. From the decorations on these pots we learn something about the people.
- Show the children the dishes of sand and tell them that within the sand, are the remains of some Ancient Greek pottery. In pairs, the children must carefully find and remove the pottery, by digging gently with spoons, and sweeping away the sand with brushes.
- When they have found all the pieces, they should try to put them together to make the pot and think about what the pictures say about everyday lives of Ancient Greeks. The children can write down or talk about what they think the pictures mean.

Extension

The children could make a model plate by drawing and cutting out a large circle or oval from card. They should then decorate it with scenes from life today. The images could be coloured in just one colour, such as red or orange. Encourage the children to swap their finished plates and see if they can identify the objects or activities depicted. The plates could form part of a wall display, along with the assembled 'pottery'.

AGES 5–7

Objectives

- To appreciate the skill of an archaeologist.
- To assemble pieces of 'pottery' to make the whole object.
- To find out about the Ancient Greeks by interpreting scenes on pottery.

Subject references

History

- Identify different ways in which the past is represented. (NC: KS1 3)
- Find out about the past from a range of sources. (NC: KS1 4a)
- Ask and answer questions about the past. (NC: KS1 4b)

Science

- Find out about a material and how it was chosen for its uses on the basis of its properties. (NC: KS1 Sc3 1d)

Art and design

- Represent observations and make images and artefacts. (NC: KS1 2c)

Lesson 2 Statues and figures

AGES 7–9

Objectives
- To appreciate the skill of an archaeologist.
- To see how pottery can provide information about the Ancient Greeks' way of life.
- To see how statues and figures can provide information about the Ancient Greeks' way of life.

Subject references
History
- Recognise that the past is represented in different ways. (NC: KS2 3)
- Find out about people from an appropriate range of sources such as pictures and artefacts. (NC: KS2 4a)
- Ask and answer questions and select and record information relevant to the focus of the inquiry. (NC: KS2 4b)

English
- Speak audibly and clearly, using standard spoken English in formal contexts. (NC: KS2 1e)

Art and design
- Select and record from first-hand observation. (NC: KS2 1a)
- Design and make artefacts. (NC: KS2 2c)

Resources and preparation
- For the Starter photocopy page 13 onto card, and cut out the pottery items. Cut each item into many parts, depending on the age or ability of the children, and bury each set of parts in a shallow dish of dry sand. For the main activity: photocopy page 14 onto card and cut out the statues and figures. Again cut up each item into many parts, depending on the age or ability of the children, and bury each set of parts in a shallow dish of dry sand.
- Each pair of children will need: a dish with the buried pottery, a spoon and a brush, paper and pencils. More confident learners will need a lump of Plasticine® or self-hardening modelling clay.

Starter
Tell the children that we know a great deal about the Ancient Greeks from the artefacts they left behind. Present the class with the four dishes of 'pottery', and tell them that there are believed to be some artefacts buried in the sand. Arrange for four groups of two children to act as archaeologists and carefully dig out the pieces. When this task is complete, let some of the children assemble the pottery, and let the others suggest what the images on the pots are, and what they reveal about the Ancient Greeks' way of life. Record the children's ideas on the board, and return to these in the Plenary.

What to do
- Present each pair of children with a dish that contains either a statue or a figure, but do not hint what may be buried there. Tell the children to excavate and assemble the pieces carefully.
- When the pieces have been assembled, ask the groups to write down what they think the 'artefact' is and what it tells them about the Ancient Greeks.

Differentiation
- Some children may need help in assembling the artefacts, if the pieces are very small and numerous. They may need help in interpreting and extracting as much information as possible from the 'artefacts'.

- Give more confident learners some Plasticine® or modelling clay and ask them to mould a figure of a present-day person or a represention of an activity. This could be done away from the rest of the class and be presented later in the Plenary. The class should identify what the sculptures represent.

Assessment

The children can be assessed on the ease with which they assemble the pieces of the 'artefacts' and the information about the Ancient Greeks that they glean from them.

Plenary

- Ask each pair of children to report to the whole class about their findings from their pottery figures. Their answers should include the following: The soldier shows that the Ancient Greeks had good blacksmiths who could shape armour to fit the body. The Greeks may have been aggressive, and they fought with spears and shields. The man shows that simple clothing was worn and that some men had short hair and no beard. The woman shows that elegant dresses could be made, which were held together with metal pins. The plough figure shows that farmers wore simple clothes and that they could till the land, which suggests that the Greeks grew crops and kept 'work' animals. The musician shows that people sat on stools and were capable of making, playing and enjoying musical instruments. The actor may cause the most difficulty in interpretation, but steer the children towards the idea that the man is wearing a mask. You may have to provide more information from the notes on page 8.
- Return to the notes made in the Starter and compare the children's responses to the pottery, with the information on page 8.
- If statues have been made, they can be exhibited and the children can assess their accuracy in representing the present day.

Outcomes

- The children can appreciate that care and skill is needed in recovering, assembling and interpreting artefacts.
- The children can use artefacts to provide information about life in an earlier age.

Did you know?

The *Colossus of Rhodes*, statue of the god Helios, was over 34m tall! It was the 7th wonder of the world.

Lesson 3 Ancient Greece

AGES 9–11

Objectives
- To use grid references to identify the positions of settlements in Ancient Greece.
- To plot routes around the Greek Empire.
- To place the Ancient Greeks and the modern Olympics on a timeline.

Subject references
Geography
- Use maps and grids. (NC: KS2 2c)
- Describe where places are. (NC: KS2 3c)
- Recognise how places fit within a wider geographical context. (NC: KS2 3g)

History
- Place people into correct periods of time. (NC: KS2 1a)
- Find out about people from documents (maps). (NC: KS2 4a)

Mathematics
- Solve time problems. (NC: KS2 Ma2 4a)

Resources and preparation
Each child will need a photocopy of page 15. For the Extension, each pair of children will need nine small cards, 6cm x 4cm.

What to do
- Issue copies of page 15 and draw attention to the mountainous nature of Ancient Greece, shown in Map 1.
- Point out the labelled sites (city states or important sites) on Map 1 and ask the children whether these places are situated on the mountains or on the land in between them. Having established that the places are on low-lying land, let the children work out the grid references for all the places on the map. For example, Elis is D4 and Sparta is G8.
- Discuss how and why Ancient Greeks might have used the coast and rivers in preference to travelling through the mountains.
- Tell the children that the Ancient Greeks set up trading settlements in many distant places, and that athletes, from these places, came to take part in the Olympic Games.
- Ask the children to plot, on Map 2, routes to Olympia, that athletes might have taken. Greek ships tended to stay close to the coast when possible (athletes travelling from Kyrene would come straight across the Mediterranean Sea and Naucratians would sweep across the Mediterranean Sea between Rhodes and Crete). The children should realise that athletes travelled long distances to compete in the games.

Extension
- Write the following time periods on the board, in random order, and ask the children to write down each time period, on separate pieces of card:
World War II 1939–1945, Anglo Saxons 350–1066, Egyptians 5000BC – 332BC, Vikings 700–1066, Ancient Greeks 1500BC – 393AD, Ancient Olympic Games ended 393AD, Tudors 1485–1603, Victorians 1837–1901, Modern Olympic Games began 1896, Romans 753BC – 476AD, Ancient Olympic Games began 776BC.
- Let the children arrange the time periods to construct a timeline. They will need to put the dates relating to the Olympic Games below the Ancient Greek card and the Victorians card. They could calculate the time period during which the Olympic Games took place in Ancient Greece (see page 8) and the time from the end of the ancient games to the beginning of the modern ones.

Ancient Greek pottery

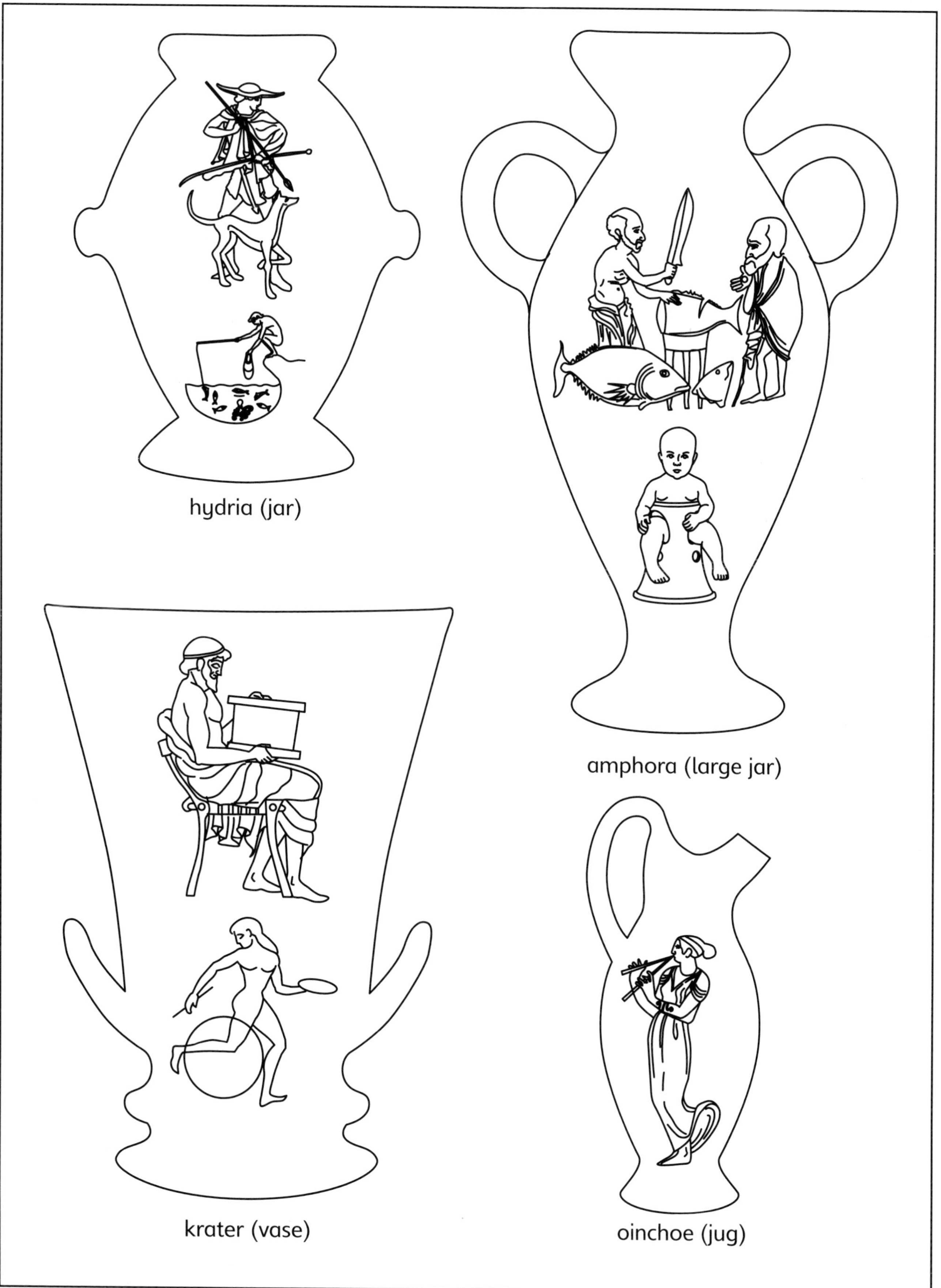

Statues and figures

Ancient Greece

Map 1

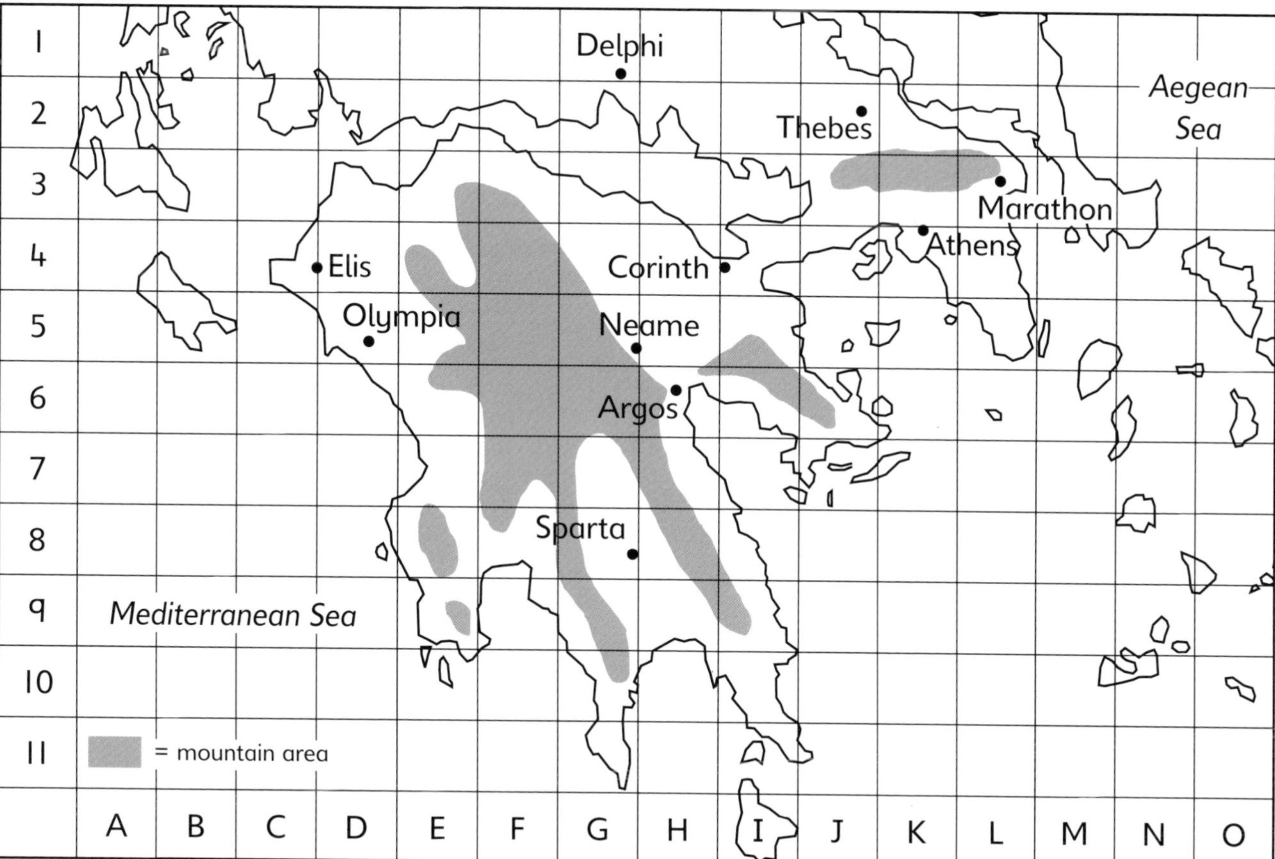

Map 2

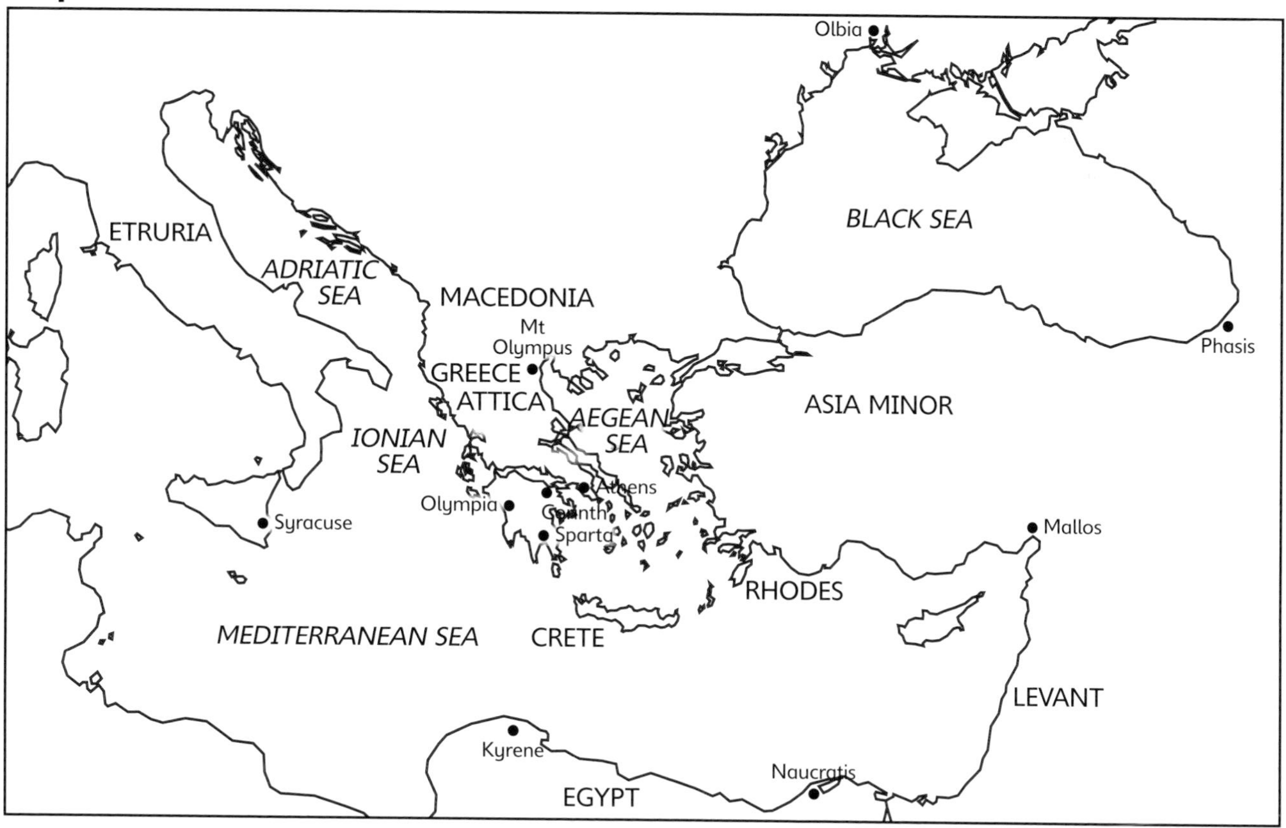

Theme 2

Life in Ancient Greece

BACKGROUND

Houses in Ancient Greece were made of dried-mud bricks. Wealthy people lived in houses built around a courtyard. For security, there were often no windows on outside walls and any existing windows, had shutters. The Greek word for burglar was 'wall- digger' as this was how they broke into houses!

A house could have a kitchen, dining room, bedrooms and a room where the women wove cloth. The courtyard was a place for the children to play and it also had a shrine. Wealthy families had slaves who would cook, clean and supervise the children. They would also collect water, either from a well in the courtyard, or from a fountain in town.

Food was prepared in the kitchen, and people ate with their fingers and a spoon. Popular foods were eggs, grapes, olives, figs, honey, cheese, chickpeas, beans, cabbage, garlic, leeks, lentils, lettuce, onions, peas, apples, plums, pears, nuts, fish (such as tuna, sea bass, eel, anchovies and sardines), prawns, squid, chicken, goose and pheasant.

IMAGE © SANKLAI/STOCKXCHNG

When an animal was sacrificed to the gods, the meat was served at a feast. Deer and boar were scarce, so they too were only eaten after sacrifice. Bread was widely eaten and was often dipped in water or wine.

Each Ancient Greek god controlled some aspect of human life, so people worshipped particular ones. At the shrines in homes, offerings such as food and wine were made.

Temples would house a statue of a god. Worship (including sacrifices) took place at an outside altar.

THE CONTENTS

Lesson 1 (Ages 5–7)
A Greek home

The children learn about Ancient Greeks' homes, draw wall pictures to represent Greek life and assemble a model home.

Lesson 2 (Ages 7–9)
A Greek temple

The children assemble a temple and design and make a god to fit inside it.

Lesson 3 (Ages 9–11)
Gods and letters

The children learn about the Olympian gods and the Greek alphabet. They make words and appreciate that some information about Greek life has been gathered by studying their writing.

Notes on photocopiables
A Greek home (page 21)

Here are two sides of a home, and a shrine. Two photocopies are needed to assemble the home. Make sure that the children draw before cutting out and know which are the outside and inside walls.

A Greek temple (page 22)

The sheet shows two sides of a temple and an altar. Two sheets are needed to assemble the temple. The children will need to make their own roofs from card.

Gods and letters (page 23)

This provides information about the gods. It also contains the Greek alphabet.

Lesson 1 A Greek home

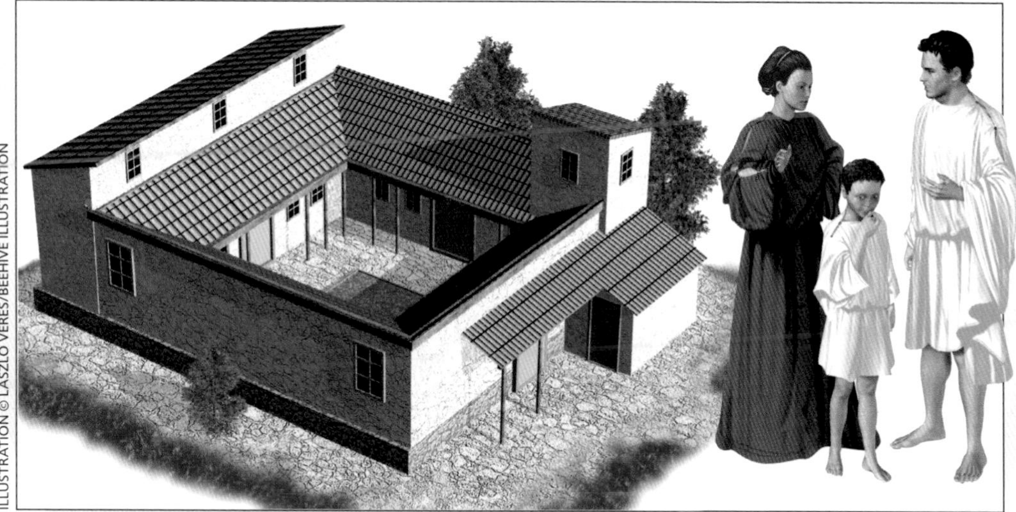
ILLUSTRATION © LASZLO VERES/BEEHIVE ILLUSTRATION

AGES 5–7

Objectives
- To learn about the way of life in Ancient Greece.
- To construct a Greek home and relate its features to the way of life.

Subject references

English
- Remember specific points that interest them. (NC: KS1 En1 2b)

History
- Find out about the past from a range of sources. (NC: KS1 4)

Mathematics
- Solve a problem by using simple tables and charts to classify information. (NC: KS1 Ma2 5a)

Science
- Understand that eating the right food helps humans to keep healthy. (NC: KS1 Sc2 2c)

Resources and preparation

- Make a model home before the lesson. Cut out the first section on page 21, fold lines 1–2 and 3–4 at right angles, and stand the section up, as in diagram A. Cut out and fold the second section, as above. Bend all the X and Y tabs, at right angles, so that X slots against the inside wall of the next section, and Y slots against the outside wall, as in diagram B (a top view). Keep the two roof tabs flat. Glue all the tabs in place. Cut out the sections from a second photocopy and join as before, (see diagram C). Cut out a shrine from one of the photocopies and fold it, as in diagram D. Place the shrine inside the quadrangle.
- Each child will need: two photocopies of page 21 on thin white card, scissors and glue (enlarge if required).

What to do

- Tell the children about the lives of Ancient Greeks and show them the model home you have made, pointing out and explaining the shrine. Tell the children that they are going to make a house too but they are going to add something to it: they are going to put drawings on the walls showing everyday activities. (These can include, on the inside: children playing, a slave carrying water, women watching the children; and on the outside: men going to work, even a burglar trying to break in.)
- Let the children work in pairs to assemble the home. Tell them to make their drawings before assembling the home. (A Greek man and child are included to show the children how they can make their drawings.) Children may like to add a simple decorative border to the top of the shrine.
- Arrange the finished homes together to create a village. You may also like to include a temple (see Lesson 2).

Extension

- List some of the foods that the Ancient Greeks ate (see page 16). Find out how many children in the class eat each item. The children could present the data as bar charts using the categories: vegetables, fruit, seafood and meat.
- Examine and assess the Ancient Greek diet. The diet was balanced, with meat, dairy, vegetables and fruit, and lacked large amounts of starchy foods such as potatoes (which had not yet been seen in the Western world). The Greeks also used olive oil, which today often forms part of a healthy diet.

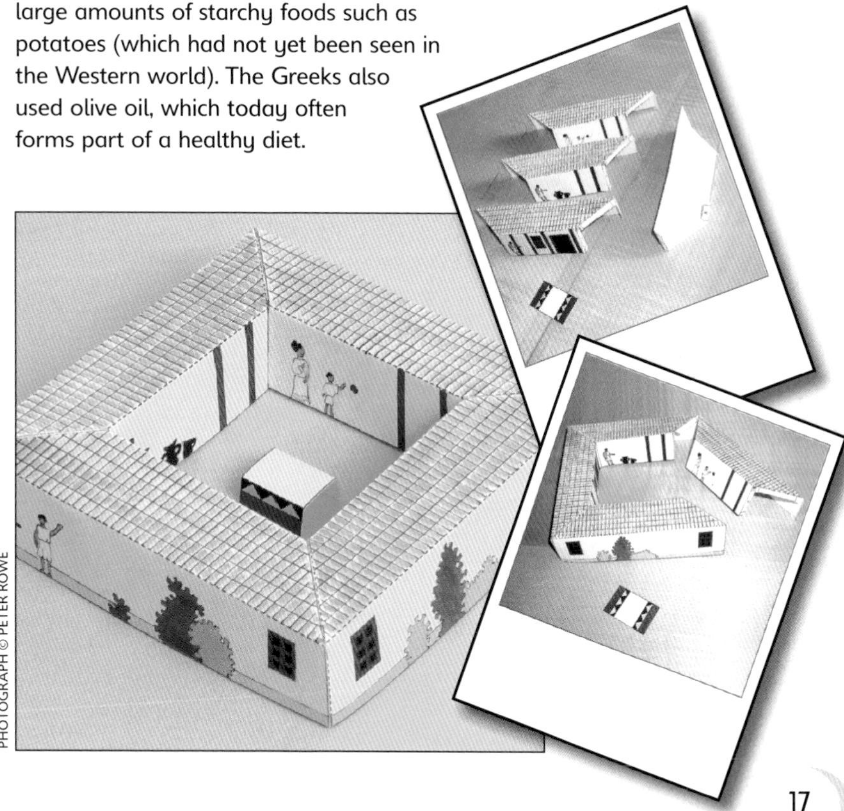
PHOTOGRAPH © PETER ROWE

Lesson 2 A Greek temple

AGES 7–9

Objectives
- To learn about the way of life in Ancient Greece.
- To construct a Greek temple.

Subject references

English
- To speak audibly. (NC: KS2 En1 1e)

Science
- Know the importance of a varied diet. (NC: KS2 Sc2 2b)

History
- Learn about beliefs and attitudes of (people) in the past. (NC: KS2 2a)
- Find out about people from historic buildings. (NC: KS2 4a)
- Study the way of life and beliefs of people living in Ancient Greece. (NC: KS2 12)

Art and design
- Make an artefact. (NC: KS2 2c)

Design and technology
- Measure, mark out, cut and combine components accurately. (NC: KS2 2d)

Resources and preparation

- Each pair will need: two photocopies of page 22 on white card, scissors, glue, Plasticine® or self-hardening modelling clay, sheets of cardboard, rulers. You will also need: a model Greek home and shrine (see Lesson 1). Classroom assistants or voluntary helpers will be needed to assist in supervising the children as they work and giving advice.
- You may like to make a sample step using diagrams 2a and 2b as a guide. The step should be larger than the base of the temple and the corners cut out, so that the tabs can be folded in and glued to hold the folded edges of the step together, at the corners (see photographs on page 19).

Starter

- Show the children the model home and tell them that wealthy people lived in such buildings. Talk to the children about the lives of Ancient Greeks – see the information in the Background section on page 16. Talk about the rooms in the home, furniture, food, the role of women, role of men and slaves.
- If you are linking the topic with health issues you may like to digress a little, and look at the diet of the Ancient Greeks. Ask the children to assess their diet for its healthiness. They should conclude that it was a healthy diet.

What to do

- Point out or remind the children that each home had a shrine where the family would worship a particular god. Show the children the small shrine you have made, which fits into the courtyard of the home. Explain that Greek towns or cities had temples, which were considered to be the homes of the gods. Explain that the gods were also worshipped at these temples. Tell the children that they are going to make their own model temple.
- Hand out copies of page 22 and let the children work in pairs to assemble the temple. Go through the whole procedure with them first:

1) Each sheet contains a temple side and an end, and so two sheets are needed to make the walls.
2) They will need to construct a roof from card, and may like to take measurements and cut it out, before they assemble their temple. Point out the roof supports, in diagrams 1a and 1b.These should be made from strips of cardboard, folded lengthways, at right angles, and glued into position. The supports should hold the roof in place so

IMAGE © MELISSA LEEKE

Did you know?

The Ancient Greeks sacrificed oxen, horses, sheep, chickens and fish in honour of the gods.

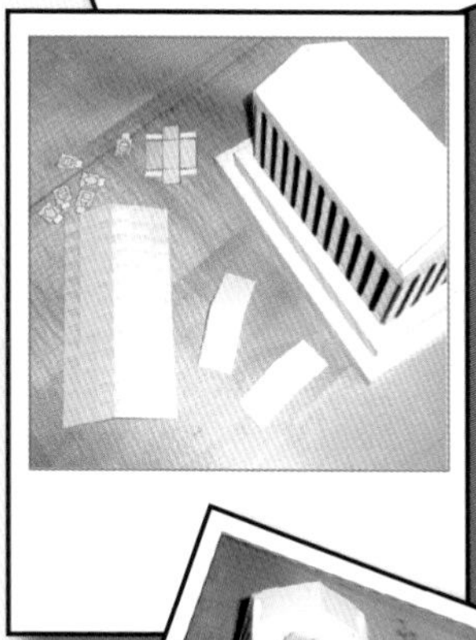

that it can be lifted off.
3) The temple contained a large statue of a god (the god was thought to have lived inside the statue). A statue can be made in a standing or seated position, and should be put, inside the temple, before the roof is placed.
4) The altar is to be assembled and placed outside the temple as shown in diagram 3. This would have been used for making animal sacrifices as part of worship.
5) The temple was in an elevated position and steps were used to enter it. Show the children the step that you have made and explain how to make the corners.

- Let the children work out a plan to make their temple and god. They should check it with you before they start work. If the plan is satisfactory let the children build their temple.

Differentiation

- More confident learners may like to research Greek gods before they make their models. They may like to choose a particular picture of a god, to help them make an accurate model.
- Some children may need help with planning and measuring. They may also prefer to make a simple figure to serve as a god.

Assessment

The children can be assessed on the thoughtfulness of their plans, the way they work together, the quality of their model god and the assembly of the temple.

Plenary

Let the children set up their temples and allow some of them to demonstrate how the roof can be removed to reveal the god. Encourage them to talk about some of the characteristics of their god.

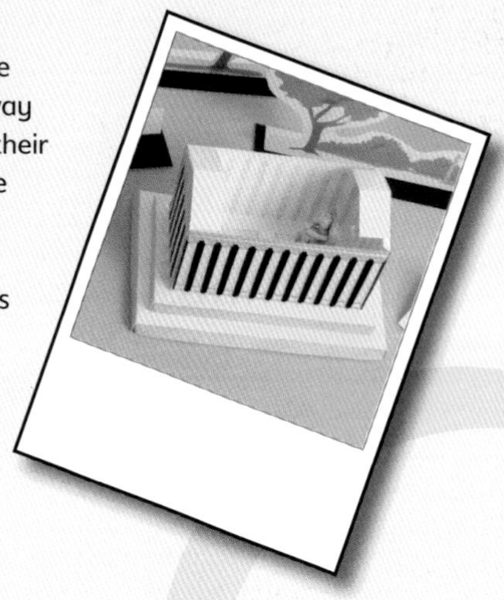

Outcomes

- The children learn about the everyday life of the Ancient Greeks.
- The children work safely together to construct a model temple.

Lesson 3 Gods and letters

AGES 9–11

Objectives

- To learn about the gods who lived on Mount Olympus.
- To understand that the Ancient Greeks had an alphabet which can be used to convey information.

Subject references

History

- Learn about the characteristic features of the periods and societies studied, including the ideas and beliefs of men, women and children in the past. (NC: KS2 2a)
- Learn about Ancient Greek gods and goddesses, and beliefs. (NC: KS2 12)

PHOTOGRAPH © ALLISON PARRY

Resources and preparation

Each child will need a photocopy of page 23. They will also need books with pictures of Ancient Greek statues of the gods.

What to do

- Tell the children that the Ancient Greeks believed that their lives were influenced by a range of gods. Show some pictures of gods and goddesses. The Ancient Greeks believed that twelve gods lived on Mount Olympus – the highest mountain in Greece.
- Hand out photocopiable page 23 and ask the children to look at what each god or goddess was responsible for. Why do they think people worshipped them? For example, a farmer would worship Demeter in hope of a good harvest.
- Ask the children to work out how some of the gods were related (for example, brothers, sisters or sons and daughters of Zeus).
- Point out the Greek alphabet and ask the children to use it to spell their names and then the names of gods.
- Explain that knowledge of the language and the alphabet is needed by historians in order to understand Ancient Greek writing.

Extension

You may wish to include the following details to illustrate how the gods were regarded. If the children have studied the Romans, you could link the Greek and Roman gods.

Name	Notes	Roman version
Zeus	Olympic Games held in his honour. Mountain tops and eagles were sacred.	Jupiter
Hera	Sacred place was Argos; sacred birds were peacock and cuckoo.	Juno
Poseidon	Lived in the sea. Dolphins sacred. Isthmian games in Corinth held in his honour.	Neptune
Hades	Grim-faced god. West considered sacred as it's where the Sun sets and appears to enter Hades.	Pluto
Demeter	Demeter was the goddess who protected the growing crops so that there could be a good harvest.	Ceres
Aphrodite	Formed from waves, stepped onto land in Cyprus. Sacred flower was rose.	Venus
Ares	Always took with him into battle his sons Phobos (meaning fear) and Deimos (meaning panic).	Mars
Artemis Apollo	They were twins.	Diana
Athena	Sprang from Zeus' head when it was struck with an axe. Owl featured on coins in Athens.	Minerva
Hermes	Escorted ghosts of the dead to the boatman who ferried them across the Styx to Hades.	Mercury
Hestia	She eventually left Olympus.	Vesta
Dionysus	Sometimes took the form of a bull.	Bacchus

A Greek home

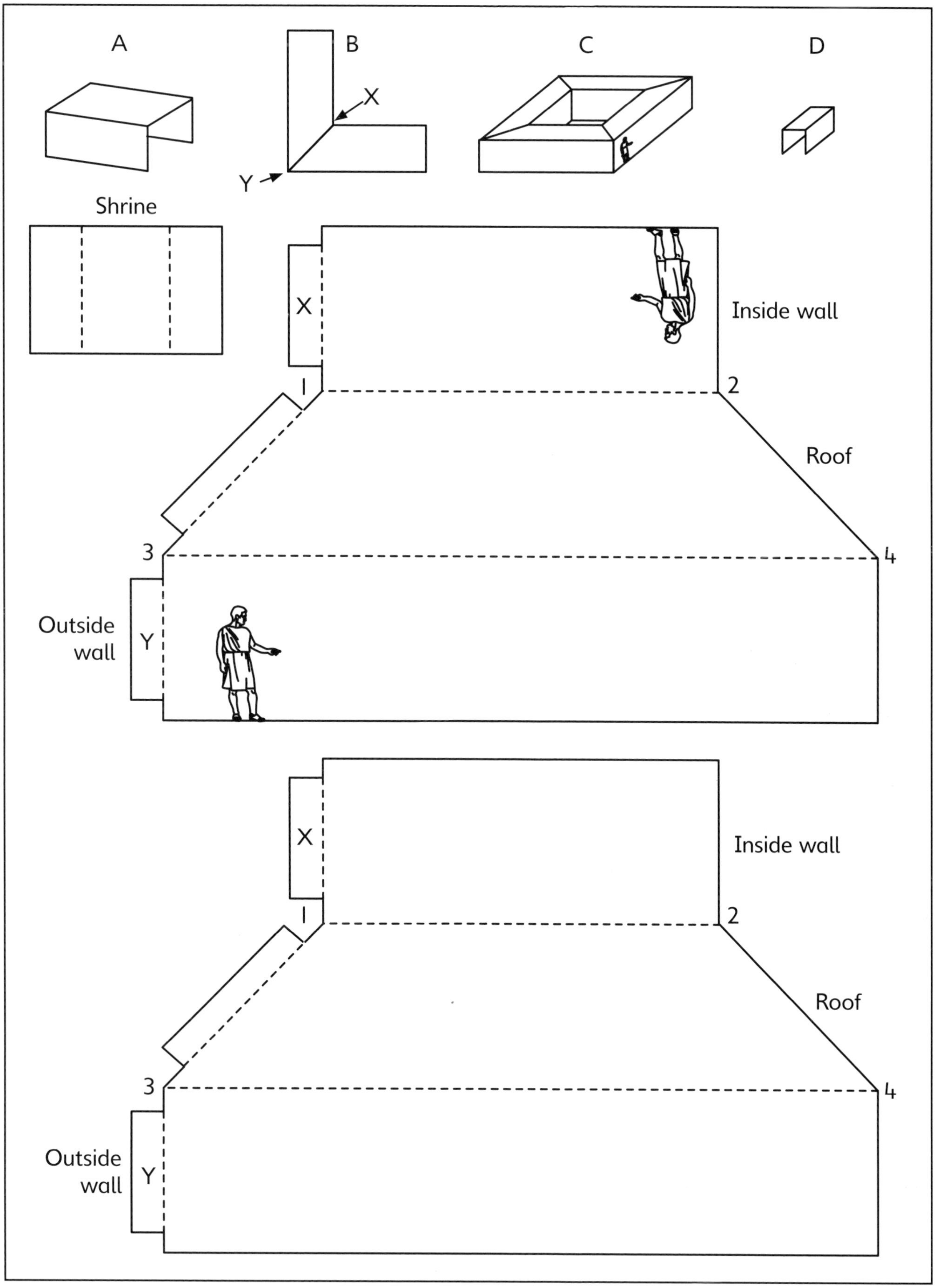

A

B

X

Y

C

D

Shrine

X

Inside wall

1

2

Roof

3

4

Outside wall

Y

X

Inside wall

1

2

Roof

3

4

Outside wall

Y

A Greek temple

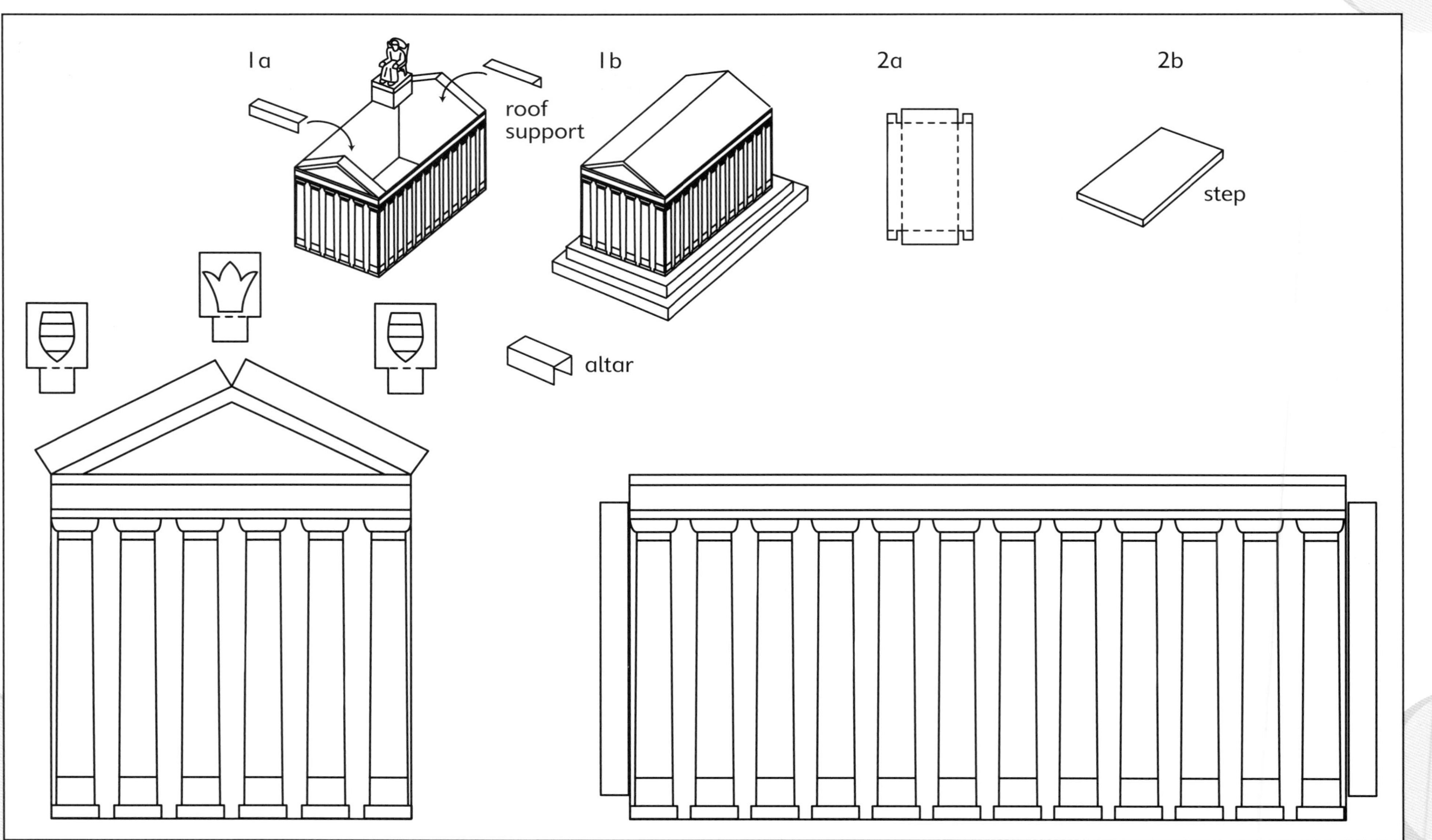

Gods and letters

The gods of Olympus

Zeus	Ruler of the gods and god of the sky. He showed his displeasure by causing thunder, lightning and rain.
Hera	Zeus' queen (and also his sister) and goddess of women and marriage.
Poseidon	The god of the sea and of earthquakes – brother of Zeus.
Hades	God of the dead and ruler of the underworld – brother of Zeus.
Demeter	Goddess of crops and harvest. Sister of Zeus.
Aphrodite	Goddess of love and beauty.
Ares	God of war. Son of Zeus.
Artemis	Goddess of the wild, the Moon and hunting – daughter of Zeus.
Apollo	God of the Sun, archery, music, healing and prophecy. Son of Zeus.
Athena	Also called Athene; the city goddess of Athens, goddess of war and wisdom.
Hermes	The messenger of the gods and god of travellers. Son of Zeus.
Hestia	Goddess of the hearth (the fireplace) worshipped to protect the home – sister of Zeus.
Dionysus	God of plants, wine and pleasure. Son of Zeus.

Greek alphabet

α alpha a	β beta b	γ gamma g	δ delta d	ε epsilon e	ζ zeta z
η eta e	θ theta th	ι iota i	κ kappa k	λ lambda l	μ mu m
ν nu n	ξ xi x/ks	ο omicron o	π pi p	ρ rho r	σ,ς sigma s
τ tau t	υ upsilon u	φ phi t/ph	χ chi ch	ψ psi ps	ω omega o

Theme 3

Going to the games

BACKGROUND

The games were held every four years. In the spring of an Olympic year, three heralds were sent across the country to announce a truce between any fighting states, enabling people to travel safely to the games. It is thought that only free boys and men could take part in or watch the games. Each city had two open buildings where their athletes trained for ten months – the palaistre for boxers and wrestlers, and the gymnasium for runners and throwers.

The games took place on the second full moon, after the summer solstice. On their way a spectator might see athletes, food sellers, jugglers, musicians, donkeys, oxen being led for sacrifice and men carrying tents.

The important places at Olympia were:

- Temple of Zeus – held a 12-metre statue of him, in gold and ivory
- Temple of Hera
- Bouleuterion – the organising council's building which held the altar of Horkios Zeus, where the athletes were sworn in
- Philippeon – a monument to the rulers of Macedonia
- Leonidaion – hotel for officials
- Baths – where athletes could relax
- Palaestra – for wrestling, boxing and jumping
- Gymnasium – for throwing and running
- Prytaneion – where the eternal flame was kept and the winners celebrated
- Treasuries – temples for offerings to gods
- Zanes – 16 bronze statues of Zeus served as a reminder to obey the rules (paid for by the fines of cheating athletes)
- Krypte stoa – arched entrance through which athletes passed into the stadium
- Stadium – race track which held 45,000 spectators
- Hippodrome – track for chariot and horse racing, which was three times the length of the stadium, with a sharp bend at each end
- Sacred olive tree – where branches were cut to make the winners' wreathes.

IMAGE © ALLISON PARRY

THE CONTENTS

Lesson 1 (Ages 5–7)
Preparing for the games

This can introduce the link between health and exercise. The children consider how their body changes during exercise. They learn that athletes trained for the games, and also practise a simple skill for a competition.

Lesson 2 (Ages 7–9)
Olympia

The children draw a picture of people going to the games. They label a picture of Olympia. They consider the features they would have seen, on a walk through Olympia.

Lesson 3 (Ages 9–11)
The games of Greece

The children learn about the five major games held in Ancient Greece and measure the distances between the sites.

Notes on photocopiables
Preparing for the games (page 29)

This features scales for measuring breathing, heartbeat and body temperature, to be used during a warm-up and a throwing game.

Olympia (page 30)

This picture shows the main areas of Olympia, with labels to be cut out and arranged.

The games of Greece (page 31)

This map features Olympia, Isthmia, Delphi, Nemea and Athens, together with information about the origins of the games and the sequence in which they took place.

Lesson 1 Preparing for the games

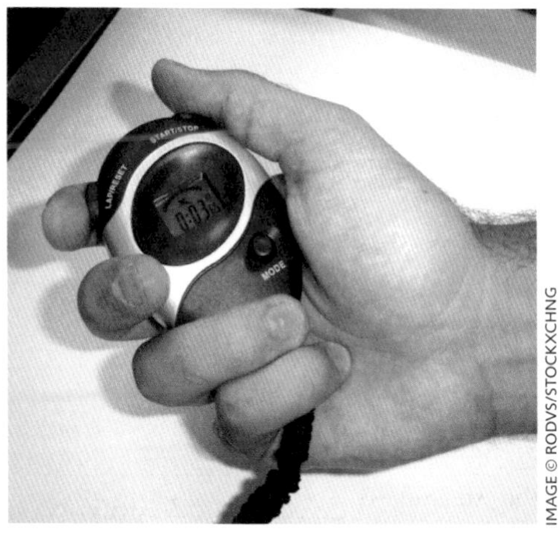
IMAGE © RODVS/STOCKXCHNG

Resources and preparation

- Each child will need: a copy of photocopiable page 29, a beanbag and two hoops of different sizes. You will need: a suitable space for the exercises; a metre ruler or sports tape to mark out the throwing position.
- This lesson can lead into Theme 5, Lesson 1 'To crown a champion'.

What to do

- The human body is designed to be active; exercise helps to keep it healthy. If muscles (including the heart) are not used, they become weak. Exercise also helps blood flow and bone and joint strength.
- Tell the children that they can measure how exercise changes the body. Breathing can be monitored by placing one hand on the stomach and one on the chest, and feeling if breaths are slow and shallow or fast and deep. Heartbeat can be monitored by putting one hand at the bottom of the breast- bone and feeling for a slow, weak beat or fast, strong beat. Temperature can be monitored by observing physical signs such as a change of colour or perspiration, or by feeling the forehead.
- Give out photocopiable page 29 and ask the children to assess their body scales before warm up. Tell them to circle the number that they think describes their breathing, heartbeat and temperature.
- Explain that both the body and the mind need to be prepared for exercise and this can be done by some simple warm up activities. Let the children try raising and lowering legs and arms, gentle jogging and a six-to-ten-second body stretch.
- Ask the children to measure and record their breathing, heartbeat and temperature again. They should notice that they have all risen.
- Explain that after vigorous activity, the body should also be cooled down by activities such as walking, walking on tiptoe, slow jogging and whole-body stretching.

Extension

- Tell the children that the athletes who competed in the Olympic Games trained and practised for ten months, and athletes today train for most of the year.
- Demonstrate how to throw a beanbag underarm. Let the children try it a few times then set out hoops as page 29 shows. Ask the children to throw the beanbag ten times with each hand and record the score each time. They could take a few practice throws, then record their scores again.

Did you know?

The word 'athlete', in Ancient Greek means, 'one who competes for a prize'.

IMAGE © 2007/JUPITER IMAGES CORPORATION

AGES 5–7

Objectives

- To notice how the body changes during exercise.
- To learn about the importance of warming up and cooling down.
- To practise underarm throwing.
- To record results in a table to monitor progress.

Subject references

Physical education

- Repeat simple skills and actions with increasing control and co-ordination. (NC: KS1 1b)
- Recognise and describe how their bodies feel during different activities. (NC: KS1 4b)

Science

- Know that taking exercise helps humans to stay healthy. (NC: KS1 Sc2 2c)

Mathematics

- Use a table to organise information. (NC: KS1 Ma2 5a)

Lesson 2 Olympia

AGES 7–9

Objectives
- To learn about the people who attended the Olympic Games.
- To learn about the site at Olympia.

Subject references
History
- Identify characteristic features of societies including attitudes and experiences of men, women and children. (NC: KS2 2a)
- Find out about events from an appropriate range of sources. (NC: KS2 4a)
- Learn about the way of life and beliefs of people living in Ancient Greece. (NC: KS2 12)

English
- To imagine and explore feelings and ideas, focusing on creative uses of language and how to interest the reader. (NC: KS2 En3 9a)

ILLUSTRATION © LASZLO VERES/BEEHIVE ILLUSTRATION

Resources and preparation
Each child or group will need: photocopies of pages 13–15 for reference, and a copy of page 30, paper, a sheet of white card about A3 size, scissors, pens, rulers and glue.

Starter
Use the background information on page 24 to tell the children about when and how often the Olympic Games took place and who attended them. Show the children the pictures on photocopiable pages 13 and 14 for reference and ask them to draw a picture on a piece of paper (landscape orientation) showing people going to the games. Take in the copies of pages 13 and 14 before moving onto the next section.

What to do
- Issue copies of photocopiable page 15 and look at the position of Olympia on both maps. Note that Map 2 shows that Olympia is a great distance from Mount Olympus (where people might think the games were held). Point to other places in Greece and the colonies, outside the country, where athletes and spectators came from. End by saying that the Olympic Games were the most important sporting event of the Ancient world and continued for 1169 years.
- Take in photocopiable page 15, and issue photocopiable page 30. Tell the children that Olympia was originally a farming area. The site was a beautiful area of countryside where two rivers met – one small, fast and gushing, and the other large and slow flowing. A conical hill covered in pine trees gave the area extra charm and atmosphere, and, it wasn't long before the local people considered it to be a very special place.

Some people believed that Zeus wrestled with Kronos (his father – also a god) for the control of the world. On winning, Zeus arranged for other gods to take part in contests at Olympia, to celebrate the event. Others believed that when Prince Pelops defeated a king and became king himself, he set up the games there, to thank Zeus. A third belief was that Hercules (or Herakles as he was known by the Greeks) set up the games to celebrate the end of his Labours.

- Go on to explain that the original site of the Olympic Games was eventually destroyed by earthquakes and was covered in mud when the rivers flooded. Archaeologists in the 19th century began to uncover the site, and the picture on the photocopiable sheet shows how they think Olympia looked at the time of the games.
- Ask the children to cut out the picture and mount it in the centre of a white piece of card so that there is a broad border in which to paste the labels.
- Then ask them to cut out the labels, paste them in appropriate places on the border and draw lines from the labels to the features on the picture.
- Now ask the children to imagine that they are athletes. Which buildings would they pass on their way from the gymnasium to the stadium? (Taking the shortest route, the Philippeion, prytaneion, Temple of Hera and treasuries.)
- Ask the children to imagine that they are wealthy spectators staying at the Leonidaion. Which buildings would they pass on their way from the Leonidaion to the stadium? (Temple of Zeus, bouleuterion and hippodrome.)

Differentiation

- Ask more confident learners to write an imaginative account of what it might have been like to travel along the road to Olympia. Who might they have met? What might it be like travelling with a crowd?
- Some children may need help placing the labels on photocopiable page 30, so that the label lines do not cross. They may also need help in making sure the label lines reach the correct features.

Assessment

The children can be assessed on the quality of and detail in their drawings and also on the clarity and accuracy of their labelling.

Plenary

- Mount the pictures of the crowds from the Starter, in a line on the wall, to generate the idea that a large number of people attended the games. Mount some of the labelled pictures of Olympia below them.
- By now, the girls have probably commented on the lack of females at the games! Explain that females were not allowed to attend (if they did they would be thrown off a cliff) but had their own games called the Heraea games. These were also held at Olympia and may have been held in the same year as the Olympic Games. They were a form of worship to Hera. Girls and women took part in races on a track that was five-sixths the length of the track used by men. They wore a crown of olive leaves and ate meat from cattle, sacrificed to the goddess.

Outcomes

- The children know about the people who attended the Olympic Games.
- The children can identify features of Olympia.

Lesson 3 The games of Greece

AGES 9–11

Objectives

- To learn about the important sporting events in Greece.
- To learn about the reasons for the games.
- To learn about the development of athletics and sports in the Ancient world.

Subject references

History

- Study the beliefs and achievements of people living in Ancient Greece and the influence of their civilisation on the world today. (NC: KS2 12)

Geography

- Use a map with a scale. (NC: KS2 2c)

English

- Obtain specific information through detailed reading. (NC: KS2 En3 3c)
- Imagine and explore ideas focusing on creative use of language and how to interest the reader. (NC: KS2 En2 9a)

IMAGE © ALLISON PARRY

Resources and preparation

Each child will need a copy of photocopiable page 31 and a ruler (or a piece of string).

What to do

- Give out copies of photocopiable page 31 and let the children read about the origins of sport. If the children have studied the Egyptians or Sumner (in Mesopotamia) you may wish to talk about some of the things they learned in the context of sport, and see what they can remember.
- Write the following questions on the board (answers are given in brackets):

1) In which countries have archaeologists found the earliest evidence of athletics and other sports? (Egypt and Mesopotamia.)
2) By the time of the Olympics, which athletics/sports events were already taking place? (Archery, acrobatics, ball games, boxing, horse riding, rowing and wrestling.)
3) How many games took place in Ancient Greece? (Hundreds – four main ones.)
4) Which was the first games to take place in the four-year cycle shown? (Isthmian.)
5) What were the four most important games held in Greece and which gods did they honour? (Olympic – Zeus; Pythian – Apollo; Isthmian – Poseidon; Nemean – Zeus.)
6) Use a ruler and the map scale to find the distance in a straight line from a) Olympia to Mount Olympus, b) Elis to Olympia, c) Athens to Elis, d) Delphi to Elis, e) Olympia to Nemea. (a) 275km b) 25km c) 175km d) 100km e) 75km.)

- Let the children find the answers from the text and the maps. (Less confident learners may prefer to use the larger-scale map and a piece of string to measure some of the distances. *NB the larger-scale map does not show Mount Olympus or Athens.*)

Extension

- Encourage the children to imagine that they are Greek athletes, taking part in the different games, from 480BC to 476BC. Ask them to place a pencil tip on Isthmia, move it to the site of the next games and continue their travels until Olympia, in 476BC.
- Read the Background section on page 24. Ask the children to use this information and the exercise above, to write a short account of what it might have been like to be an athlete in Ancient Greece.

Preparing for the games

Body scales before warm up

Breathing rate

1	2	3	4	5

very slow — very fast

Heartbeat

1	2	3	4	5

very slow — very fast

Body temperature

1	2	3	4	5

very cold — very hot

Body scales after warm up

Breathing rate

1	2	3	4	5

very slow — very fast

Heartbeat

1	2	3	4	5

very slow — very fast

Body temperature

1	2	3	4	5

very cold — very hot

Beanbag throw

Left-hand throw	Score	Score	Right-hand throw
1			1
2			2
3			3
4			4
5			5
6			6
7			7
8			8
9			9
10			10

Olympia

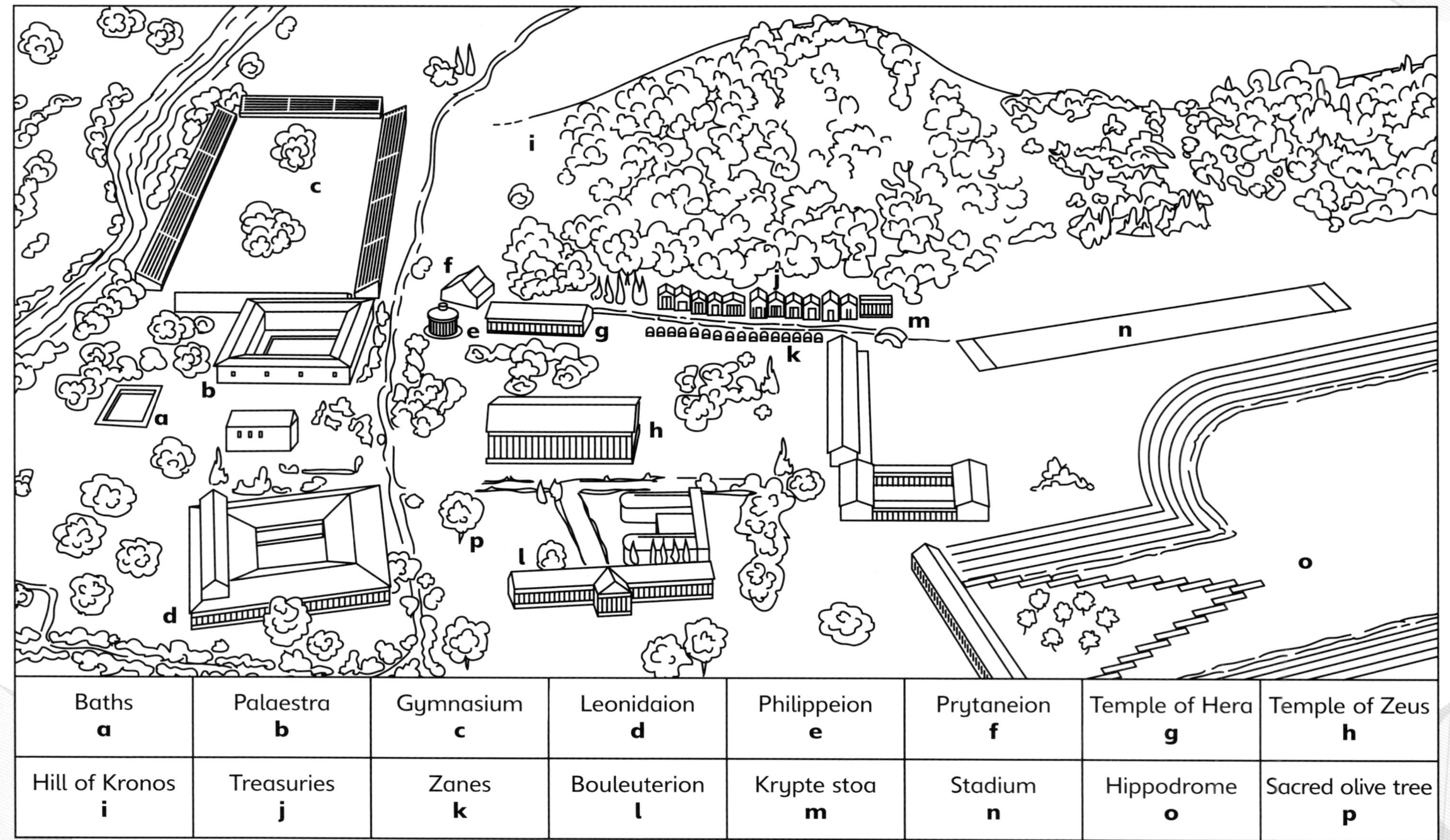

Baths **a**	Palaestra **b**	Gymnasium **c**	Leonidaion **d**	Philippeion **e**	Prytaneion **f**	Temple of Hera **g**	Temple of Zeus **h**
Hill of Kronos **i**	Treasuries **j**	Zanes **k**	Bouleuterion **l**	Krypte stoa **m**	Stadium **n**	Hippodrome **o**	Sacred olive tree **p**

The games of Greece

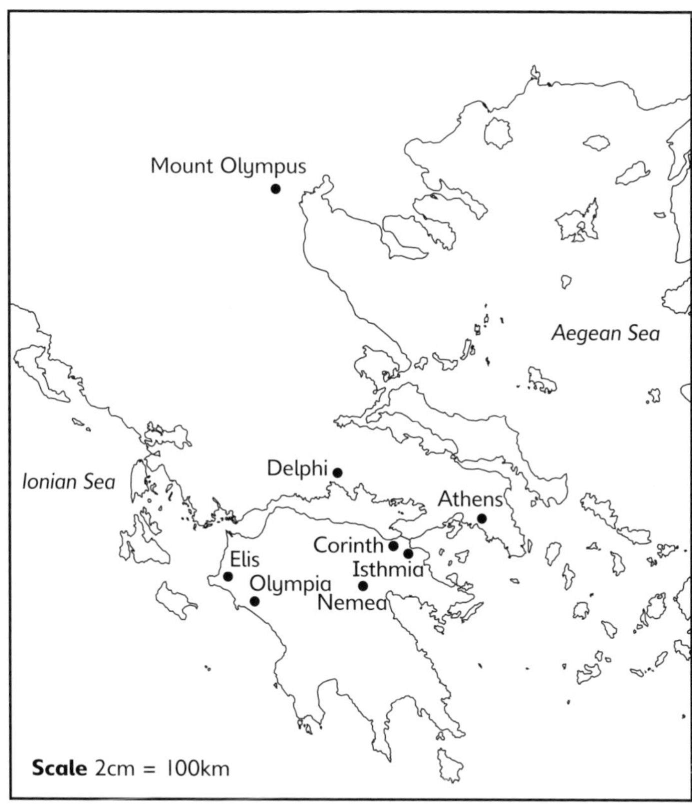

The major games of Ancient Greece during a four-year period

Games	Month held	Year held (BC)
Isthmian	April	480
Olympic	August	480
Nemean	August	479
Isthmian	April	478
Panatheniac	August	478
Pythian	September	478
Nemean	August	477
Isthmian	April	476
Olympic	August	476

The start of sport

The Ancient Greeks did not invent athletics and sport. Archaeologists have found evidence of archery, acrobatics, ball games, boxing, horse riding, rowing and wrestling, in Mesopotamia and Egypt, over two thousand years before the Olympic Games began. Five hundred years before the Olympic Games, people in Greece raced on foot and with chariots. Hundreds of cities and towns held games. Games were held to honour a god, and were part of a religious festival. There were four very important games. The Olympic Games were the first to be established, to honour Zeus. The three other important games were, the Pythian games at Delphi to honour Apollo, the Isthmian games at Isthmia to honour Poseidon and the Nemean games at Nemea, also to honour Zeus. The Panatheniac games in Athens honoured Athena.

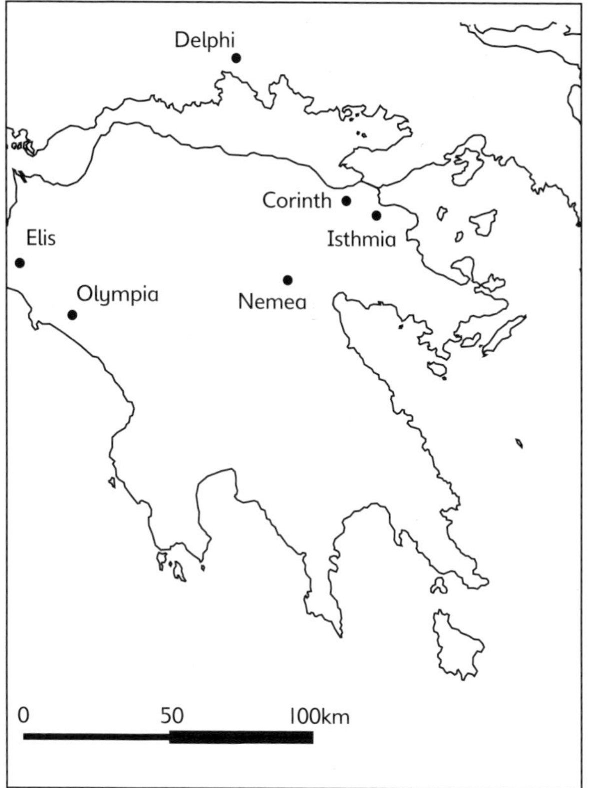

Theme 4

The ancient games

BACKGROUND

The first Olympic Games took place over one day, and featured running races only. In time, it developed into a five-day event. Before the games started, a boy was selected to use a golden sickle to cut one leafy branch, for each event, from an sacred olive tree. Each branch was made into a winner's crown. The five-day schedule might have taken the following form:

Day 1 Morning: Athletes sworn in at the Altar of Horkios Zeus. (They had to assure the officials that they had practised for ten months and that they would obey the rules, not cheat or use magic!) Athletes then went to another altar and made a sacrifice to Zeus, Hermes, Apollo or Hercules and prayed for success. Boys' contests held. Afternoon: Musical events, tours of Olympia.

Day 2 Morning: Procession of horses and chariots to the hippodrome, chariot racing, horse racing. Afternoon: Pentathlon. Evening: Winners' parade; singing of victory songs.

Day 3 Morning: Procession to the Temple of Zeus, led by ten officials in purple robes. The sacrifice of 100 oxen to Zeus. Afternoon: Running races. Evening: Banquet with the meat of the sacrificed oxen.

IMAGE © ALLISON PARRY

Day 4 Morning: Wrestling. Noon: Boxing and pankration (a mixture of boxing and wrestling). Afternoon: Hoplitodromos (25 athletes ran two lengths of the stadium carrying a shield and wearing a helmet).

Day 5 Morning: Winners' procession and crowning. Afternoon and Evening: Feasts and celebrations.

THE CONTENTS

Lesson 1 (Ages 5–7)
Olympic sports

The children make card figures of athletes. When all the cards are stood up, the children get a sense of how busy Olympia was during the games.

Lesson 2 (Ages 7–9)
A Chariot

The children identify the Olympic sports and how winners were rewarded. They make and race a chariot.

Lesson 3 (Ages 9–11)
The chariot race

The children learn about events at the Olympic Games. They make and race chariots.

Notes on photocopiables

Olympic sports (page 37)

The sheet shows: line 1) boys running, wrestling and boxing; line 2) chariot racing, horse racing; line 3) discus, javelin, jumping, running; line 4) men wrestling, running and boxing; line 5) pankration, hiplotodromos and prize giving. The Π (pi Greek letter for p) on five of the pictures, indicates that these sports were part of the pentathlon. Athletes in Ancient Greece competed naked, rather than in the short tunics used here. Boxers did not wear gloves; they tied leather thongs around their hands. No saddles or stirrups were used for horse riding.

A Chariot (page 38)

This provides the chariot chassis and wheels – two for the chariot, and two with whirls to represent the horses' legs and feet as they race along.

The chariot race (page 39)

This provides the four horses, the front and sides of the chariot and the charioteer.

Lesson 1 Olympic sports

Resources and preparation

- Each child will need: a photocopy of page 37, 14 pieces of card about 6cm x 9cm, two pieces of card about 9cm square (depending on the size of children's handwriting), scissors and glue.
- Write the names of the sports (from the notes on the photocopiables) on a board and hide them before the lesson. You will also need: ten cards with a 32cm-long footprints on them, sports tape, A4 card (optional).

What to do

- Tell the children about the different sports at Olympia (see the notes on page 32). See if the children can identify the sports on photocopiable page 37. Let the children cut out the pictures.
- Issue one of the larger cards and show the children how to stick the picture of the chariot racer at the top, leaving plenty of space underneath it. Ask the children to follow your example.
- Check the children's pictures are at the top of the cards, then issue the second large card and ask them to stick the horse rider to the top of it. Check these, then let the children continue with the rest of the (smaller) cards.
- Reveal the words on the board and relate them to each picture. Ask the children to write the words on their cards.
- When all the sports have been labelled, ask the children to fold the bottom of the card so that it stands up. They should have a group of busy athletes before them.
- Talk about some of the similarities and differences between these athletes and those of today.
- Each child could stick the bases of their athletes onto A4 card. Arrange these on a side table to show a busy Olympic scene.

Extension

- Tell the children that the Ancient Greeks believed a man called Hercules (Herakles in the Greek) performed many tasks which required great strength such as, wrestling a lion or changing the path of a river. In order to celebrate one of these tasks, Hercules organised the first race at Olympia. The track in the stadium at Olympia was based on 600 of Hercules' footspan. Hercules was believed to be a large man with feet 32cm long (making the track 600 x 32cm = 192m long).
- Show the children the ten cards of Hercules' footprints. Ask one child to put them, heel-to-toe, along the floor and let the children make a similar line with their own feet. Measure the distance covered by ten Hercules' feet, then measure out a distance six-times this length. Explain that the stadium was 100 times longer!
- If the school field is large enough, measure out 192 metres to show the children how far the athletes ran. Some races were one length, some were two and some were up to 24 lengths. You may wish to develop this activity into measuring with non-standard units.

AGES 5–7

Objectives

- To learn the different sports that took place at Olympia.
- To see similarities and differences between athletes of Ancient Greece and those today.

Subject references

History

- Identify differences between ways of life at different times. (NC: KS1 2b)
- Learn about past historical events, for example the Olympic Games. (NC: KS1 6d)

Lesson 2 A chariot

AGES 7–9

Objectives

- To learn about the different sports that took place at Olympia.
- To make a chariot and race it.

Subject references

Design and technology

- Cut materials and assemble, join and combine components and materials accurately. (NC: KS2 2d)
- Reflect on the progress of their work as they make, identifying ways they could improve their products. (NC: KS2 3a)

Physical education

- Gain knowledge about athletic activities. (NC: KS2 5e)

Resources and preparation

Each child or group will need: card photocopies of pages 37, 38 and 39, scissors, glue, two plastic straws, a ruler, pencils, a broad gentle slope (made of thick cardboard, covered in newspaper, for example, which will provide friction to help wheels to turn). Additional classroom assistance would be helpful.

Starter

Give out copies of page 37 and ask the children to identify the different sports shown. (Use the information on page 32 to check their answers.) Go on to say that some athletes took part in the pentathlon and point out that the sports in this section are marked with the Greek letter for p, in the lower left corner. Explain that *pente* is Greek for *five* and that *athlon* means *contest*: there are therefore, five events in a pentathlon. Ask the children to tell you what sports they would do if they were taking part in the pentathlon. Point out that Ancient Greek winners received a prize of an olive wreath. Tell the children that they are going to have an opportunity to win a contest by making and then racing their own chariot.

What to do

- Talk about how long the Ancient Olympic Games lasted, and tell the children that chariot racing took place on the second day of the games.
- Give out card copies of photocopiable pages 38 and 39 and let the children cut out the chassis and wheels on page 38.
- You and your adult assistants should make small holes in the circles marked on the long sides of the chassis, and in the centre of the wheels, for the children.
- Let the children enlarge the holes so that a pencil can almost pass through them. (It is better if the children make the holes a little too small at first and enlarge them carefully

Did you know?

The materials used to make chariots were wood, bone, ivory, bronze, iron, copper and leather.

later when they test the holes with the straws.)

- Tell the children to fold in the sides of the chassis and bend and glue the tabs to turn the chassis into a box-like structure.
- The children can now cut out the horses, sides of the chariot and charioteer, from photocopiable page 39. The tab of each horse should be bent and glued to one of the four parallel lines on the chariot. The sides of the chariot and its tabs should be bent and glued onto the lines of the rectangle, behind the horses. The tab at the foot of the charioteer should be bent and glued on the line behind the chariot.
- Now ask the children to cut two straws to a length of ten centimetres. They should push each straw in turn through the holes in the chassis. Advise the children that the holes should be large enough to let the straws turn freely.
- The wheels should then be attached to the ends of the straws. The children should enlarge the wheel holes gradually, until the ends of the straws make a tight fit in them.
- Suggest that the chariot should be tested to make sure that the wheels turn freely and do not fall off easily. (They can be raced in the Plenary.)
- Explain that Greek chariot races were very dangerous. Anything up to 60 chariots competed together over a number of laps of the hippodrome. The numbers of chariots competing, the speed they travelled and the tight turns of the circuit meant that many chariots overturned and crashed into each other.

Differentiation

- More confident learners could add threads for reins connecting the hands of the charioteer with each of the horses' heads. They could consider ways to improve the design, such as making an alternative wheel and axle assembly.
- Some children may need help with cutting out and constructing, but it is not important to cut around the horses' ears. Children may need help in successfully attaching the wheels to the axles.

Assessment

The children can be assessed on the quality of the construction of the chariots.

Plenary

Let the children hold a chariot race by letting the chariots roll down a broad, gentle slope. They should hold several races and record the result each time. Award five points for first, four for second, three for third, two for fourth and one point for fifth. The winner is the one with the highest number of points after all the races have been completed.

Outcomes

- The children know the different sports that took place at Olympia.
- The children can make a chariot and race it.

Lesson 3 The chariot race

AGES 9–11

Objectives

- To learn about how events in the Ancient Olympics were organised.
- To design and make a programme of events for the Olympic Games.

Subject references

Physical education

- Gain knowledge about athletic activities. (NC: KS2 5e)

Design and technology

- Cut materials and assemble, join and combine components and materials accurately. (NC: KS2 2d)
- Reflect on the progress of their work, identifying ways they could improve their products. (NC: KS2 3a)
- Generate ideas for products after thinking about what they will be used for. (NC: KS2 1a)
- Use finishing techniques to improve the appearance of their product. (NC: KS2 2e)

English

- Use features of layout, presentation and organisation effectively. (NC: KS2 1d)
- Inform, focusing on subject matter, conveying sufficient detail for the reader. (NC: KS2 9b)

PHOTOGRAPH © PETER ROWE

Resources and preparation

- Each child will need: a photocopy of page 37, five sheets of A4 paper (which the children can cut down when they have decided how to arrange the pictures), scissors and glue, pencils, reference books and/or internet access.
- For the Extension, each child or group will need: model-making resources as for Lesson 2 (see page 34). Alternatively, offer a selection of materials and objects, such as boxes, cardboard, wood strips for axles, drawing pins for holding wheels, for the children to design and make their own chariots. Provide photocopiable page 23 and reference books showing Greek chariots.

What to do

- Give out copies of photocopiable page 37 and ask the children to identify the sports. (Use the information on page 32 to check their answers.)
- Tell the children that some athletes took part in the pentathlon, indicated by Π (pi), the Greek letter for 'p'. Explain that *pente* is Greek for *five* and *athlon* means *contest*. Elicit that there are, therefore, five events in a pentathlon. Tell or remind the children that winning athletes would receive an olive wreath as their prize.
- Discuss the likely sequence of events at the Olympics (see page 32). How does this compare with the modern Olympics? Encourage the children to carry out their own research.
- Ask the children to design and make a programme for the five Olympic days, in booklet form. Encourage them to use their research and the pictures on page 37, which they can cut out. Note that Day 2 has a large number of pictures associated with it.

Extension

The children can make the chariots on photocopiable pages 38 and 39 and race them as in Lesson 2. Alternatively, children could make their own chariots and race those. They might think of names for their chariots and write them on the sides of the chassis using the Greek alphabet on photocopiable page 23. As in Lesson 2, ask the children to hold several races to find an overall winner.

Olympic sports

A chariot

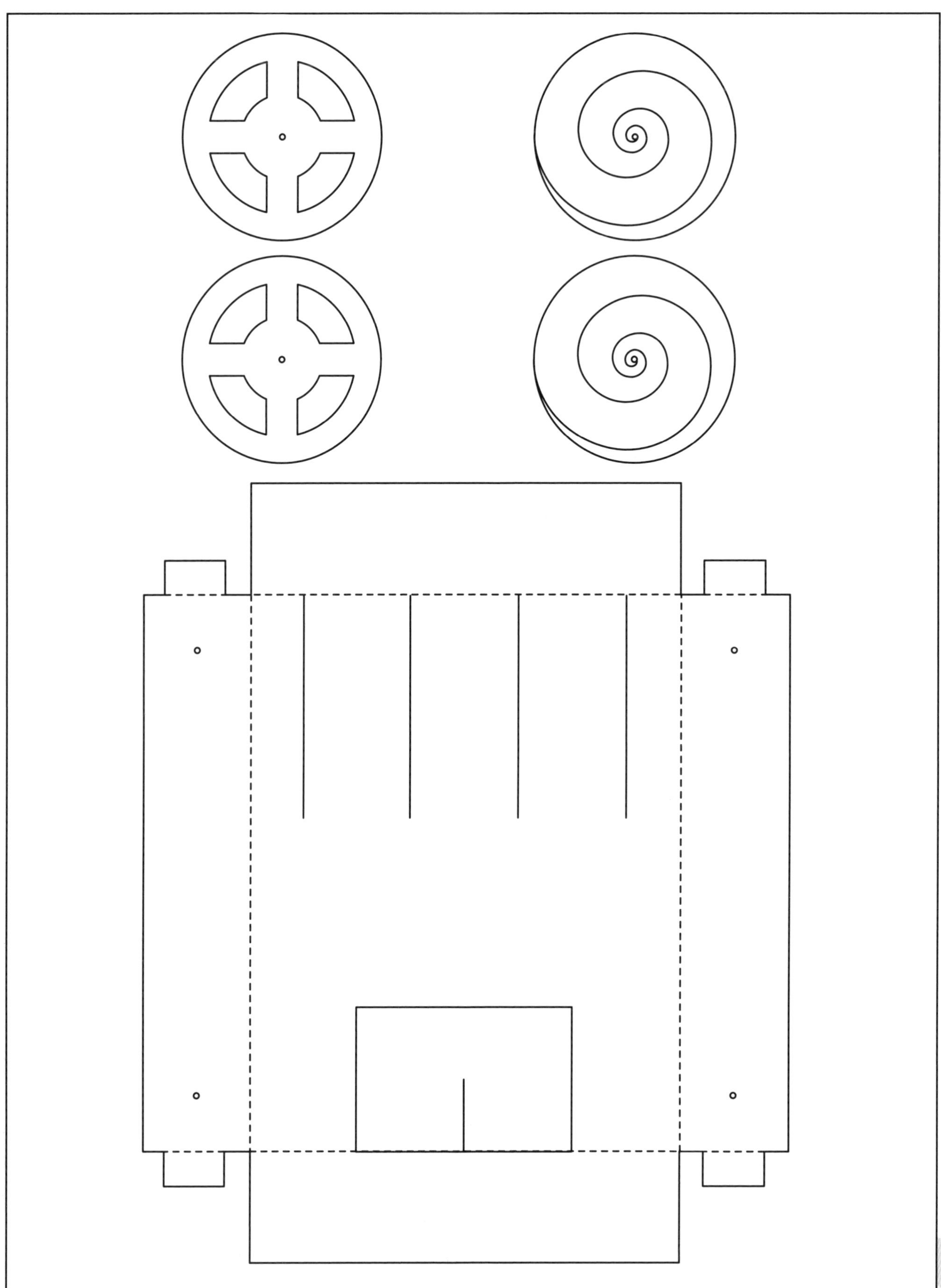

The chariot race

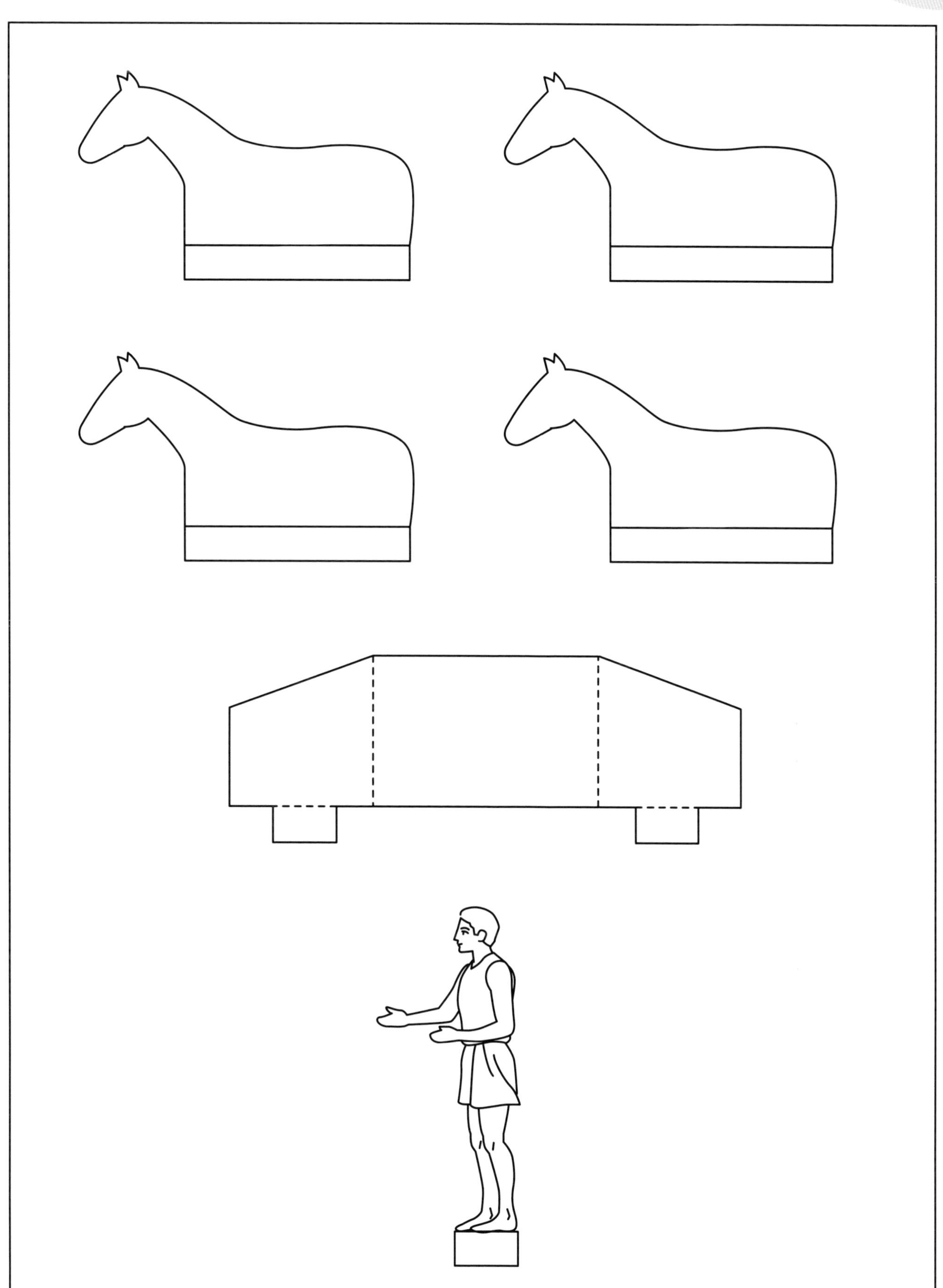

Theme 5

Ancient to modern

BACKGROUND

The theme of winning and being a champion is the focus of Theme 9, but it is introduced here to round up the ancient games. Winners' wreaths at Olympia were from a sacred olive tree. At the Pythian games, the wreaths were laurel; at the Isthmian games, they were pine; at Nemea, wild celery, and at Athens they were olive.

There were many changes to Olympia during its long use as a sporting venue. When Alexander the Great became the ruler of Greece, he had statues of himself and his family erected there. When the Romans conquered Greece, Augustus had a shrine built as if he were a god. The land was shaken by earthquakes, and some buildings were destroyed. Floods covered the land with mud. The games continued, though, until the Roman Emperor Theodosius came to power. He banned the worship of non-Christian gods and the games stopped. In the fifth century, a great earthquake destroyed all the buildings and then, in the sixth century, Olympia was covered in mud again. In time, the area became farmland and the ruins remained buried for over 1000 years.

A principle at the heart of the modern Olympic movement is good sportsmanship. Good athletes keep to a schedule of practice and improvement, follow the rules, respect and congratulate competitors, and keep an even temper.

IMAGE © STEVE PASTON/ ACTION IMAGES

THE CONTENTS

Lesson 1 (Ages 5–7)
To crown a champion

The children learn about the different wreaths made for the ancient games and make an olive wreath. They have a throwing competition and devise an award ceremony.

Lesson 2 (Ages 7–9)
From old to new

The children hear and answer questions about the end of the ancient Olympics and the origins of the modern games.

Lesson 3 (Ages 9–11)
The modern Olympics

The children read and answer questions about the beginnings of the modern Olympics. They record how the number of countries entering the games has changed and consider the notion of sportsmanship. They think about how to organise a games event for the school.

Notes on photocopiables
To crown a champion (page 45)

These outlines of olive leaves can be used to make an olive-wreath crown.

From old to new (page 46)

This sheet provides a brief account of the change to the new games. Answers: 1) They were too poor and people had too little time and energy. 2) Archery, wrestling and running. 3a) 41, b) 81, c) 86. 4) Running and long jump. 5a) Held every year, b) 40. 6a) 12, b) 27, c) 33, d) 74. 7) To improve people's health and fitness.

The modern Olympics (page 47)

This is a simple account of the establishment of the modern Olympic Games, with questions. The word countries is used for simplicity, but the IOC recognises nations which may be part of a country (such as Hawaii). The statistics given are for nations. Answers: 1) It would make pupils healthy and prepare them to live and work more happily. 2) Olympia was being excavated. 3) He set up the IOC; his ideas formed the basis of the Olympic Charter. 4) 1896 in Athens. 5) 9 (a marathon is an athletic event). 5a) Cycling, fencing, gymnastics, shooting, swimming, tennis and weightlifting. 7) These years were during world wars. 8) See Background information, above.

Lesson 1 To crown a champion

AGES 5–7

Objectives
- To learn about awards at the ancient Olympics.
- To make a model olive wreath.
- To take part in a competition.
- To take part in an award ceremony.

Subject references
Design and technology
- Cut materials. (NC: KS1 2c)
- Remember and repeat simple skills and actions with increasing control and co-ordination. (NC: KS1 1b)

Resources and preparation
- The children should have tried the activities in Theme 3 Lesson 1 'Preparing for the games'.
- You will need adult assistance to make cardboard headbands for the children to attach the olive leaves to.
- Each child will need: a strip of thin, brown cardboard about 60cm long and 2cm wide, photocopiable page 45 on thin green card, scissors, glue. Each classroom assistant will need sticky tape.
- For the Extension, each group will need: a beanbag, two hoops of different sizes, a metre rule or sports tape, a hat/box, paper and A4 card.

PHOTOGRAPH © PETER ROWE

What to do
- Tell the children that the winners of the ancient Olympic Games were crowned with an olive wreath. If you have mentioned that there were other games such as the ones at Delphi or Nemea tell the children that they used different plants as explained in the background information on page 40.
- Place the cardboard strips around each child's head to measure the circumference. Once removed, cut each strip a little longer so that the ends overlap. Cover the card with tape to represent the woody part of the olive branch.
- Let the children cut out the olive leaves on the sheet and stick them onto the card ring. Encourage the children to feel like champions wearing their wreaths.

Extension
- Remind the children of their beanbag training from Theme 3. Review their performances and organise children of similar ability into groups of four.
- Tell the children that in the Greek competitions, the competitors drew lots to determine their order in the throwing events, and for pairing of boxers and wrestlers. Names were written on white wooden planks and displayed for the spectators. Ask the children to write their names on pieces of paper and put them in a hat. Let them draw the names, one at a time, to find the order of throwing. They could write down the order of throwing on A4 card and place it near where they are going to compete.
- After the competition, crown the children for first to fourth place. Say that in the ancient Olympics only the winner was crowned.

Lesson 2 From old to new

AGES 7–9

Objectives
- To learn how the modern Olympic Games began.
- To learn about how the Ancient Olympic Games ended.

Subject references
English
- Recall and re-present important features of a reading. (NC: KS2 2c)
- Obtain specific information through detailed reading. (NC: KS2 En2 3c)

Art and design
- Record from imagination. (NC: KS2 1a)
- Use a variety of methods to communicate ideas and make images. (NC: KS2 2c)

History
- Learn about the influence of the Ancient Greek civilisation on the world today. (NC: KS2 12)
- Find out about events and changes using pictures. (NC: KS2 4a)

Mathematics
- Choose and use appropriate calculations methods. (NC: KS2 Ma2 4b)

Resources and preparation
Each child will need: paper and a photocopy of page 46. Some children may need photocopiable page 23. You will also need images of Greek gods and goddesses, and of buildings with Greek columns to show to the class. For the Plenary, gather images of artefacts from Olympia and of the Olympic Games. You could also refer to images from of Olympics Games that took place during the Victorian times, such as in 1896.

Starter
- Read the account of the end of the ancient Olympic Games, in the Background section on page 40. Ask questions about it to test the children's listening skills.
- Remind the children of how the Ancient Greeks produced scenes of everyday life on their pottery, as explored in Theme 1, and ask them to draw a picture representing the demise of Olympia. The picture could include several scenes over time, such as a Roman emperor ordering people away from the temple of Zeus, an earthquake shaking the buildings to rubble while mud covers the fallen masonry, or a land where olive trees grow and goats graze.

What to do
- Give out the copies of photocopiable page 46 and read it with the children.
- Show the children pictures of Greek gods and goddesses and identify the artists.
- Then show the children pictures of buildings with Greek-style columns and ask them where they might see some like this locally. Look for answers that include banks and public buildings such as, libraries and a town halls. Discuss how Greek architecture has influenced the style of more modern buildings.
- Ask the children to work through the questions on the photocopiable sheet and write down their answers.

Differentiation
- Pairs of more confident learners could use the Greek alphabet on photocopiable page 23 to write a message to each other describing the location of two different objects in the classroom. They should then translate each other's messages and identify the object.
- Some children may need extra help in extracting the information and performing the calculations required by some of the questions on photocopiable page 46.

Assessment
The children could be assessed on their listening skills and imaginative drawing. They could also be assessed on the quality of their answers in the comprehension, and the accuracy of their calculations.

Did you know?
The *Temple of Zeus* was one of the first places to be excavated.

Plenary

- Encourage the children to make a display of the pictures they made in the Starter activity.
- Ask the children to imagine that they are archaeologists digging through the three-metre-deep layer of dried mud that covered Olympia. Show them pictures of the artefacts you have collected. Ask the children how they would feel if they were to suddenly come across the tops of these buried artefacts, and then were to dig down to reveal all of them.
- Display some images of Olympic Games that took place during the Victorian era. Look at each image with the children and remind them that they are pictures from the Victorian times. Ask for their impressions of the 1896 Olympics, from looking at the images.

Outcomes

- The children know and can visualise how the ancient Olympic Games ended.
- The children know how the modern Olympic Games began.

Lesson 3 The modern Olympics

AGES 9–11

Objectives
- To learn how the modern Olympic Games came into being.
- To compare the modern Olympic Games with the ancient Olympic Games.
- To display data as a graph.
- To formulate a concept of sportsmanship.
- To consider the issues of organising a sporting event.

Subject references
English
- Obtain specific information through detailed reading. (NC: KS2 En2 3c)

History
- Answer questions and select and record information relevant to the focus of the enquiry. (NC: KS2 4b)
- Education in Victorian Britain. (NC: KS2 11a)

Mathematics
- Represent and interpret discrete data using graphs. (NC: KS2 Ma4 2c)

PSHE and citizenship
- Know how their actions affect others; care about other people's feelings. (NC: KS2 4a) Take responsibility. (NC: KS2 5a)
- Participate in school the decision-making process. (NC: KS2 5d)

PHOTOGRAPH © PETER ROWE

Resources and preparation
Each child will need a photocopy of page 47 and a piece of graph paper.

What to do
- Review learning on the ancient Olympics and then read about the changes at Olympia in the Background notes on page 40.
- Give out photocopiable page 47, read it through and let the children answer questions 1–7.
- Discuss the statistics, and make sure the children understand that the number of participating nations increased over the period (with a slight dip in 1980).
- Once the children have plotted their graphs, ask how accurate they think it are at describing the changes. Look for an answer about it not being very accurate as it only shows venues 20 years apart.
- Ask the children to find out why there was a dip in numbers in 1980. (Some countries boycotted the games in protest of the Soviet invasion of Afghanistan.)
- The work on question 10 can be developed into a class discussion to lead into the Extension.

Extension
- Tell the children they are going to find out a little of what it was like to organise the new Olympic Games by organising a School games.
- If they are to follow the Olympic pattern, they will need a school flag to be flown or hung during the games; they may like to invent a mascot (see Theme 9, Lesson 2). Send letters home to encourage visitors to come to the games. The children will need to think about: How will the games open? – with a fanfare? Will a relay team carry a mock torch (see Theme 6, Lesson 3)? In what order will people process onto the field? Who will make the opening speech? What will the oath be and which athlete will say it? Which games/sports should be played and in what order? What will happen in the closing ceremony? Should there be another short speech? A special performance (see Theme 9, Lesson 1)?
- Let the children work in small groups and then present their ideas to the class.

To crown a champion

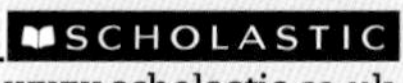

From old to new

The Ancient Greeks organised big events like the Olympic Games because their country was rich and people had time for sports. In later times, countries became poorer and people worked hard just to stay alive! They had little time or energy to organise such an event. But some sports did continue – men practised archery, wrestling was also popular and people also ran races.

Eventually, people became interested in the ancient Olympics again. William Penny Brookes was a doctor, who lived in the English village of Much Wenlock and he wanted to improve the health of his villagers. He read about the ancient Olympics and had an idea. He decided to organise his own Olympic Games called the Brookes Olympian Games and they were first held at Much Wenlock in 1850. The events included cricket, football, long jump, quoits and running. There was even a pig race and blindfolded wheelbarrow race!

Back in Ancient Greece, a man called Pausanias had written about Olympia and his books survived down the centuries. Archaeologists later read his books and found out where Olympia lay buried. In 1875, a German archaeologist called Ernst Curtius discovered the ruins. This discovery was exciting and it gave a Frenchman called Pierre de Coubertin an idea. He believed that people would be healthier if they were fitter and that starting the Olympic Games again might help. He wanted these games to be for everyone. He found out about the games at Much Wenlock and visited William Brookes, in 1890. Pierre de Coubertin was so impressed with the Brookes Olympian Games that he set up the modern Olympic Games, in which people from all over the world could compete.

The first modern Olympics Games were held in Athens in 1896. The sports were athletics, cycling, fencing, gymnastics, shooting, swimming, tennis, weightlifting and wrestling.

1) Why didn't other countries organise events as big as the ancient Olympics?

2) Name three sports which continued after the ancient Olympics ended.

3) William Brookes was born in 1809 and died in 1895. How old was he when:
a) his first games were held?
b) he was visited by Pierre de Coubertin?
c) he died?

4) Which two sports, in the Brookes Olympian Games, were also part of the ancient Olympic Games?

5) The Brookes Olympian Games were held annually.
a) What does this mean?
b) How many times had the games been held by the time Pierre de Coubertin visited William Brookes?

6) Pierre de Coubertin was born in 1863 and died in 1937. How old was he when:
a) Olympia was uncovered?
b) he visited William Brookes?
c) the first modern games took place?
d) he died?

7) Why did Brookes and de Coubertin want to set up games like the ancient Olympics?

The modern Olympics

In the 19th century, many countries thought that introducing sport into schools would make pupils healthier. They also believed that teaching sportsmanship would make people live together more happily. The excavations at Olympia were making people interested in the Ancient Greeks, and gave one man an idea. He was a wealthy French nobleman called Baron Pierre de Coubertin. He thought he could bring people, from all around the world, to compete in a modern Olympic Games. He invited people from other countries, to a meeting in Paris, in 1894 at which the International Olympic Committee (IOC) was set up.

People needed a clear idea about the purpose of the games and the way they were going to be organised. Baron de Coubertin's ideas formed the basis of the rules and regulations which became the Olympic Charter. The athletes who competed in the games had to obey the terms of this charter.

The first modern Olympic Games took place in 1896, in Athens. They were held every four years after that, except in 1916, 1940 and 1944. Athletes competed in athletics, cycling, fencing, gymnastics, shooting, swimming, tennis, weightlifting and wrestling. The marathon race was also introduced. The winner was a Greek shepherd called Spiridon Louy, who ran the 40 kilometres from Marathon to Athens in just under three hours. Women were not allowed to compete in the marathon, so the next day, a woman called Stamata Revithi ran the course as a protest.

The countries that took part in the first modern Olympic Games were Australia, Austria, Bulgaria, Chile, Denmark, France, Germany, Greece, Hungary, Sweden, Switzerland and the USA. Here are some statistics about countries that competed in the games between 1900 and 2000:

Date	Venue	Number of nations
1900	Paris	26
1920	Antwerp	29
1948	London	59
1960	Rome	83
1980	Moscow	80
2000	Sydney	200

1) Why did people think that sport in school was a good idea?

2) Why were people interested in Ancient Greece in the 19th century?

3) Why was Pierre de Coubertin important in the development of the modern games?

4) When and where did the first modern games take place?

5) How many sports were in the first modern games?

5a) Which of these sports were not played in the ancient games?

6) Make a graph to show how the number of countries, taking part in the games, changed between 1900 and 2000.

7) Why do you think the games were not played in 1916, 1940 and 1944?

8) What is good sportsmanship and what is bad sportsmanship?

Theme 6

Outdoor Olympics

BACKGROUND

This theme (and Theme 7) relate to the Summer Olympics. The Winter Olympics and the Paralympics are featured in Theme 8, Lesson 3.

One of the most well-known outdoor Olympic events is the marathon. Although it was not a feature of the ancient games, it is believed to originate in ancient legend. In 490BC a large Persian force landed at Marathon, on their way to invade Athens. The Greeks were outnumbered, so they sent a messenger called Pheidippedes to Sparta for reinforcements. The road was too rough for a horse, so it is said that Pheidippedes ran the 140 miles in two days. The Spartans could not help for a few days, until their religious festival ended; Pheidippedes travelled back with the news. The Greeks launched a successful surprise attack on the Persian army which then set sail for Athens. Pheidippedes ran from Marathon to Athens – 26 miles – to warn the Athenians, before he collapsed and died from exhaustion and battle wounds. The rest of the army followed him to Athens. The Persians were amazed at how fast they travelled and decided to retreat. The marathon race was introduced to the modern Olympics to celebrate Pheidippedes' heroic running.

The modern pentathlon is believed to be based on the deeds of a French soldier who had to get a message to his comrades. He set off on horseback, over fences (show jumping), then he fought an enemy soldier (fencing). Another enemy soldier shot his horse and he returned fire (shooting), before crossing a river (swimming) and running (cross country) to deliver the message.

The Olympic torch was lit at a ceremony at Olympia, several months before the games. A woman dressed as a priestess lit the torch with a mirror which was concentrated on the sun's rays. The torch was then carried in a relay to the opening ceremony.

IMAGE © SILBURKP/STOCKXCHNG

THE CONTENTS

Lesson 1 (Ages 5–7)
Outdoor sports

The children hear how the ancient Olympic Games ended and new games began. They make card figures of sporting activities and compare modern and ancient athletes. They learn to skip, gallop, hop, jog and run fast. They invent a running game.

Lesson 2 (Ages 7–9)
The pentathlon

The children learn about the modern pentathlon and play a board game. They take part in a triathlon and consider what it would be like to take part in the heptathlon and decathlon.

Lesson 3 (Ages 9–11)
Which outdoor sports?

The children reflect on their sporting strengths. They take part in a relay race or practise a torch relay for Olympics Day. The first part of this lesson could be used with the first part of Theme 7, Lesson 3.

Notes on photocopiables
Outdoor sports (page 53)

The sheet features archery, running, hurdling, long jump, discus, javelin, shot put, hammer throwing, baseball, canoeing, cycling, horse jumping, hockey, rowing, sailing, shooting, tennis, high jump, pole vaulting and football.

The pentathlon (page 54)

For this game, each child crosses the board as many times as they can for each event in two minutes, while their partner times them and keeps score.

Which outdoor sports? (page 55)

A list of traits needed for sports is provided. Brief descriptions of outdoor sports could help children decide which sports they might be good at.

Lesson 1 Outdoor sports

ILLUSTRATION © LASZLO VERES/BEEHIVE ILLUSTRATION

AGES 5–7

Objectives

- To learn about and identify outdoor sports that take place at the modern Olympics.
- To take part in running activities.

Subject references

English

- Attempt to write unfamiliar words. (NC: KS2 En3 2a)
- Check the accuracy of their spelling. (NC: KS2 En3 4g)
- Form letters of a regular size and shape. (NC: KS2 En3 5d)

Physical education

- Remember and repeat simple skills and actions with increasing control and co-ordination. (NC: KS1 1b)

Resources and preparation

- Select appropriate information from pages 40 and 47. Write the words for the sports on page 53 on a board and hide them before the lesson.
- Each child will need: a photocopy of page 53, 21 pieces of card about 6cm x 9cm, scissors and glue. You will also need an outdoor space, cones, beanbags and a stopwatch; an A4 sheet of card (optional).

What to do

- Tell the children about the end of the Olympic Games and the beginning of the new ones.
- Explain that in the modern games, some sports take place outside and some take place inside. In this lesson, the children are going to look at outdoor sports (avoid volleyball as it is difficult for children to identify)
- Give out copies of photocopiable page 53 and see if the children can identify the sports. Check their answers by revealing the words on the board.
- Talk about some of the sports shown. Have the children tried any of them? Are there any that are unfamiliar?
- Let the children cut out the pictures.
- Take one of the pictures and a card and show the children how to paste it at the top of the card, leaving space to write the name of the sport underneath. Show them that they will not use all the space as some of it will fold into a base so that the card can stand up.
- Let the children stick their pictures onto the cards as you have shown.
- Then ask them to write down the name of each sport on the card and check their spellings.
- The children should now fold the cards so that they stand up.
- Each child could stick the bases of their athletes onto an A4 card for Extension work in Theme 7, Lesson 1.

Extension

- Tell the children about the story of the marathon race from the background information.
- Let the children take part in some games that involve running, such as running around cones or retrieving five beanbags set out in a line. The children could run a distance, which you could time with a stopwatch, and you could even hold a race in which evenly matched runners compete, perhaps as part of an Olympics Day.

Did you know?

In 1900, American athlete, Alvin Kraenzlein, won the long jump, 60m, 110m and 200m hurdles, in Paris!

Lesson 2 The pentathlon

AGES 7–9

Objectives
- To learn about the pentathlon.
- To take part in a triathlon.

Subject references
Mathematics
- Recall addition and subtraction facts for numbers to 20. (NC: KS2 Ma2 3d)
- Use written methods to add and subtract positive integers less then 1000. (NC: KS2 Ma2 3i)

Physical education
- Take part in competitions that call for precision, speed, power or stamina. (NC: KS2 PE 10a)
- Use running, jumping and throwing skills singly. (NC: KS2 10b)

Resources and preparation
Each pair will need: a copy of photocopiable pages 53 and 54, a dice and cup, counters, paper for keeping scores. You will also need: a stopwatch, sports tape, beanbags, access to the sports field and plenty of adult support.

Starter
- Give out photocopiable page 53 and tell the children that it shows outdoor events that take place at the modern Olympic Games. Ask the children to identify the sports. Check their answers.
- Talk about some of the sports and in particular those that the children may not be familiar with, such as hammer throwing.
- Explain that some events are a combination of sports. You may like to remind them of the pentathlon in the ancient Olympics and talk about the pentathlon in the modern games, which features four alternative sports (running being common to both).
- Go on to tell the story about the origin of the modern pentathlon. Say that the sports are not suitable for children, but that they can get a sense of what it is like to compete in a multi-sport event by playing the game on photocopiable page 54. Hand out copies.
- Tell the children that the actual pentathlon has a complicated scoring system. It has been greatly simplified for this board game, but still includes the feature of subtracting points.
- Explain how to play the game. Each child takes a turn at completing each of the events on the board. Player 1 puts a counter on the first square in the shooting section. The clock is started and Player 1 shakes the dice, and moves their counter the appropriate number of squares. Player 2 writes down the number of points scored (from the square landed on) as Player 1 shakes again. Player 1 keeps moving along the first line, left to right, until two minutes are up. The total is then added up and Player 2 takes a turn.
- For the fencing event, each player's overall score is calculated by adding or deducting points from an initial 500 points. For swimming and show jumping, points are deducted from 500. In cross country, each player gets 100 points for each line completed, plus the score of the square occupied when the two minutes are up.

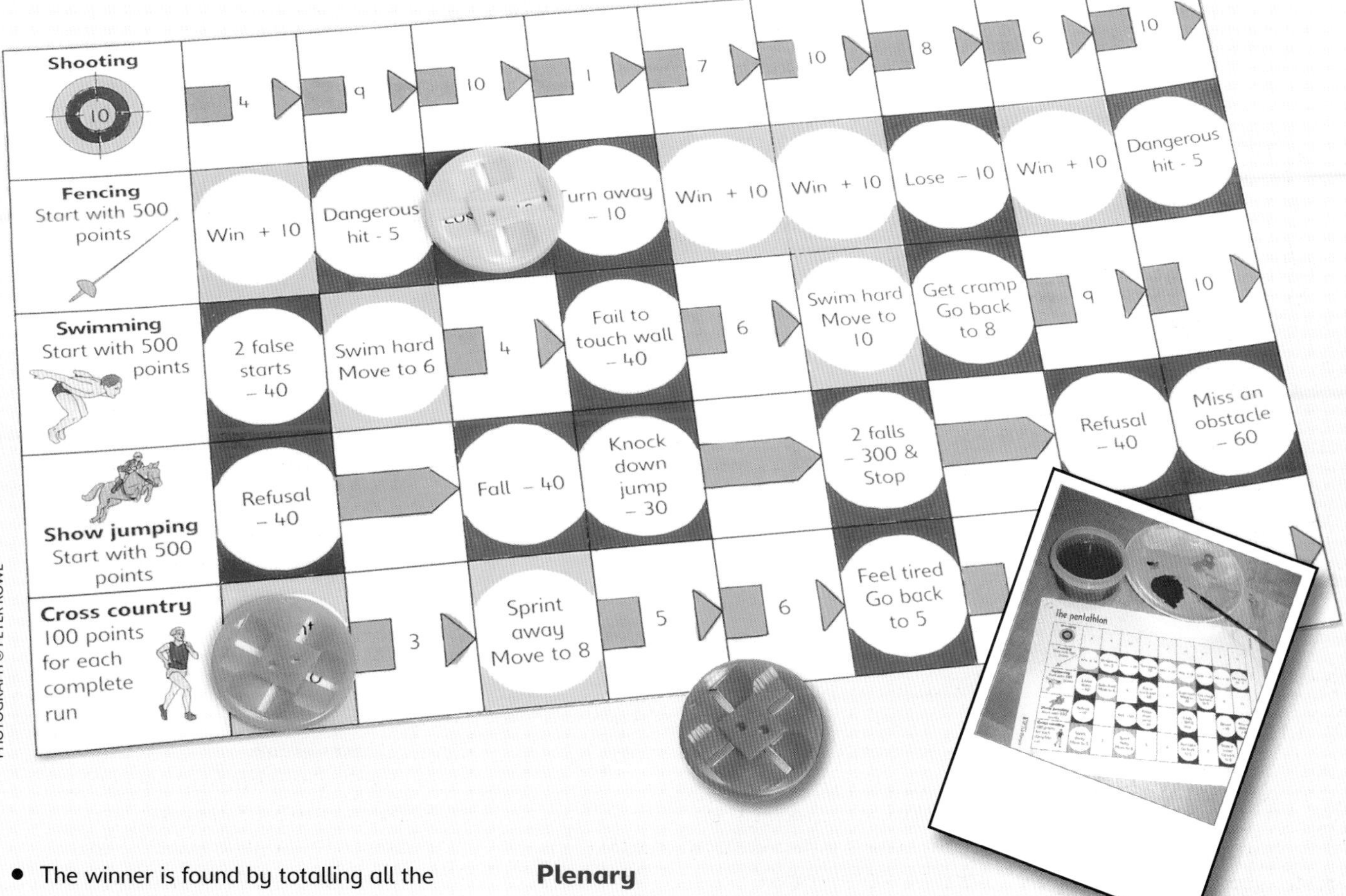

PHOTOGRAPH © PETER ROWE

- The winner is found by totalling all the scores for each event.

What to do

- Tell the children that there is also an Olympic event called the triathlon, which features cycling, swimming and running. They are going to take part in a triathlon which features running, jumping and throwing.
- Outside, coach the class in sprinting, jumping for distance and throwing for distance. Make sure the children warm up and cool down as in Theme 3, Lesson 1.
- Ask the children how points should be scored in each event and allow them to discuss and agree on a scoring system.
- Organise races, jumping and throwing events for evenly matched groups of children. This could be part of an Olympics Day.

Differentiation

- Some children will need help in scoring the board game.
- More confident learners could time the races with a stopwatch to find the fastest runner in each group.

Assessment

The children can be assessed on the way they can calculate the scores in the board game and on their attitude to training for the competitions.

Plenary

- The children could present their results for the board game and decide who should win gold, silver and bronze medals (see Theme 9, Lesson 2). Announce the results of the triathlon and the medal winners.
- Tell the children about the heptathlon (for women) and the decathlon (for men). Both take place over two days. The heptathlon consists of seven events: 100 metre hurdles; high jump, shot put and 200 metres on the first day, and long jump, javelin and 800 metres on the second day. The decathlon has ten events: 100 metres, long jump, shot put, high jump and 400 metres on the first day, and110 metre hurdles; discus, pole vault, javelin and 1500 metres on the second day. Ask the children how they would feel about taking part in such lengthy and multi-skilled events.

Outcomes

- The children can use mathematics to work out scores.
- They know the five sports in the modern pentathlon.
- They have trained for and taken part in a triathlon.

Did you know?

In the pentathlon, you have 40 seconds to fire 20 shots at a target, with an air pistol.

Lesson 3 Which outdoor sports?

AGES 9–11

Objectives
- To know about the range of Olympic outdoor sports.
- To reflect on personal sporting traits.
- To perform in a sporting team.

Subject references
English
- Make contributions relevant to a topic and take turns in discussion. (NC: KS2 En1 3a)

Physical education
- Take part in competitions that call for speed. (NC: KS2 10a)
- Use running skills singly. (NC: KS2 10b)

PSHE and citizenship
- Recognise their worth as individuals by identifying positive things about themselves and their achievements. (NC: KS2 1b)
- Understand that their actions affect others, care about other people's feelings and see their points of view. (NC: KS2 4a)

ICT
- Use simulations in order to answer *What if?* (NC: KS2 2c)

IMAGE © BOMMELI/STOCKXCHNG

Resources and preparation
- Each child will need a copy of photocopiable page 55 and internet access to http://abc.net.au/olympics/2004/kayak.htm (a kayak slalom) and http://abc.net.au/olympics/2004/skeet_shooting.htm (a shooting game). You will need a suitable outdoor space if you hold the relay races in the Extension, or a model Olympic torch.
- You may like to reshape this lesson using the first part of Theme 7, Lesson 3, having half the class considering outdoor sports and the other half considering indoor sports. A second lesson could then combine the Extensions to these two lessons.

What to do
- Ask the children to stick out their tongues and see if they can roll them up. When they find that some can do this simple feat while others cannot, discuss that everyone has different skills and characteristics and some of these can be useful in sport.
- Read the first section of photocopiable page 55 with the children. Let them write down their thoughts on their own sporting characteristics and discuss then discuss these with their friends. Be prepared for heated debates! Emphasise the point that it is natural and for everyone to be different.
- Move on to a class discussion of each sport mentioned on the sheet, considering the personal aptitudes that may be suitable. Some children may already take part in a sport and may wish to talk about it (see Extension).
- Let the children select suitable sports for themselves. Emphasise that if someone really enjoys a sport, they can work on weaknesses to make them successful competitors.
- Many sports need fast reactions. Let the children try one of the online games suggested.

Extension
- Children who participate in a sport could be invited to give a presentation about it.
- If the children have not picked out being a team player as a useful sporting trait, bring it to their attention now and say that one of the athletics events is the relay race. Divide the class into relay teams and let them practise for a race.
- Alternatively, tell the children about the torch being carried by a distance relay team from Olympia to the Olympic venue. Pass a model torch around the class. This could be performed again on Olympics Day.

Outdoor sports

The pentathlon

Shooting	**+ 4**	**+ 9**	**+ 10**	**+ 1**	**+ 7**	**+ 10**	**+ 8**	**+ 6**	**+ 10**
Fencing Start with 500 points	Win **+ 10**	Dangerous hit **- 5**	Lose **– 10**	Turn away **– 10**	Win **+ 10**	Win **+ 10**	Lose **– 10**	Win **+ 10**	Dangerous hit **- 5**
Swimming Start with 500 points	2 false starts **– 40**	Swim hard **Move to 6**	4	Fail to touch wall **– 40**	6	Swim hard **Move to 10**	Get cramp **Go back to 4**	9	10
Show jumping Start with 500 points	Refusal **– 40**		Fall **– 40**	Knock down jump **– 30**		2 falls **– 300 & Stop**		Refusal **– 40**	Miss an obstacle **– 60**
Cross country 100 points for each complete run	Sprint away **Move to 5**	3	Sprint away **Move to 8**	5	6	Feel tired **Go back to 5**	8	Stone in trainer **Go back to 6**	10

Which outdoor sports?

Everyone has skills or qualities. Here are some needed for certain sports:

- Strength
- Flexibility
- Stamina
- Fast-moving
- Quick reactions
- Good sense of balance
- Keen vision (able to see small objects at a distance).

Which do you have?

Here are the outdoor Olympic sports. What traits would each champion need? Which three sports might you be good at in the future?

Archery: Shoot arrows at a target so distant that it looks as small as this full stop.

Athletics: Running, hurdles, long jump, high jump, triple jump, pole vault, hammer, shot put, javelin, discus, heptathlon, decathlon.

Baseball: Throw, bat, catch, run.

Canoe/kayak: Paddle hard, keep balance, steer.

Cycling: Road race, time trial, BMX, mountain biking, sprinting.

Equestrian: Show great control of the horse, in dressage, show jumping and cross country.

Football: Kick, head the ball, run with it, tackle, positional sense.

Hockey: Strike a ball with a stick, pass, shoot, tackle, run with stick and ball.

Pentathlon: Shoot, fence, swim, show jump, run.

Rowing: Pull on oars quickly and/or for a long time, balance.

Sailing: Dinghies, yachts (crew of two) catamarans, windsurfing.

Shooting: With a pistol or rifle, at stationary and moving targets.

Tennis: Racket skills, serve, return, run, change direction frequently, balance.

Triathlon: Swim, cycle, run.

Beach volleyball: Teams of two in bare feet, on sand court, aim to hit a large ball over a high net; serve, dig (scoop the ball from low), set (lay up the ball), spike (downward smash shot).

Theme 7

Indoor Olympics

BACKGROUND

This Theme continues with the Summer Olympics, focusing on indoor events. Divers enter the pool from a springboard 3m high or a solid platform 10m high. The pools used for synchronised swimming have speakers that allow the swimmers to hear the music underwater, as well as out of the water.

There are three types of fencing events – *épée*, where the tip of the sword can touch any part of the opponent's body, *foil*, where it can only touch the trunk, and *sabre*, where any part of the sword can touch any part of the opponent's body. There are three fencers in a team and each one duels with each member of the opposition. The duel is fought in a space called a *piste*, 14m long x 1.5m wide. The swords are wired so that their touches are recorded electronically. Swords are blunt, but fencers wear thick protective clothing, including a mesh face mask.
Some sports have been withdrawn from the Olympics. Cricket and croquet were played in 1900; golf was played in 1900 and 1904; and polo was played five times between 1900 and 1936. Lacrosse was played in 1904 and 1908 and rugby union was played four times between 1900 and 1924. Some sports such as archery, boxing and football have been reinstated later. Triathlon and taekwondo first appeared in 2000. You may find sports in the current games which are not mentioned in this book.

IMAGE © INGRAM PUBLISHING

THE CONTENTS

Lesson 1 (Ages 5–7)
Gymnastics

The children arrange pictures of gymnastic moves in a sequence. They then practise and perform them. They also learn about other indoor events and draw pictures for a display.

Lesson 2 (Ages 7–9)
Invent a game

The children try a board game and look at ways they could change the rules. They then make up a team game to be played in school.

Lesson 3 (Ages 9–11)
Which indoor sports?

The children reflect on their sporting strengths. They consider sports that they may have an aptitude for. They take part in a relay using batons or 'torches' and try netball/basketball shooting. The first part of this lesson could be used with the first part of Theme 6, Lesson 3.

Notes on photocopiables
Gymnastics (page 61)

Here are 18 gymnastic skills, with two blank spaces for the children to draw two extra skills. The children cut out the pictures and select a few for a sequence.

Invent a game (page 62)

This is a football pitch for a simple five-a-side board game.

Which indoor sports? (page 63)

A list of traits needed for sports is given, for children to add others. Descriptions of sports can be used in conjunction with the sporting traits to help children decide which they might be good at. Note that some are combat sports or otherwise unsuitable for children (such as weightlifting).

Lesson 1 Gymnastics

Resources and preparation

- The children should have practised a range of gymnastic moves before this lesson.
- Each child will need: photocopiable page 61, scissors, glue, at least 15 cards about 6cm x 9cm. You will need: the hall or gym and suitably qualified assistants; pictures of other indoor Olympic events.
- Pictures of other indoor sports. Write the names of these sports on a board and hide them for use in the Extension.

What to do

- Remind the children that exercise is good for them and of how the body changes during exercise, as investigated in Theme 3.
- Tell them that muscles become tense when they work and soft when they relax. Ask them to extend an arm, feel their biceps and note that it is soft. Ask them to raise the forearm slowly, keep feeling the muscle and note how it changes from soft to hard as it works. Say that all muscles work like this and let the children feel their calves as they point their toes (soft) then raise their foot (hard). You may like to add that muscles are attached to the bones by tendons, and bones are connected by ligaments. When practising gymnastics, instructions must be followed to prevent these ligament tissues being damaged.
- Tell the children that they are to make a gymnastic performance from the skills shown on photocopiable page 61. They should cut out the pictures and arrange some into a sequence.
- Let each child check their sequence with you, and, if you approve, arrange for them to practise it. Remind the children that when they perform, they must remember the sequence, not rely on the pictures.
- Ask the children to perform their sequences to the class.

Extension

- Remind the children about the outdoor sports cards they made in Theme 6. Ask them to choose one picture from page 61 to represent gymnastics and mount it on card.
- Show the pictures of other indoor sports. Ask the children to draw and label their own simple pictures of these sports, cut them out and stick them onto card. Each child could mount their pictures and place them with the athletes made in Theme 6.

AGES 5–7

Objectives

- To revise gymnastic skills.
- To devise a sequence of moves then practise and perform them.

Subject references

Physical education

- Remember and repeat simple skills and actions with increasing control and co-ordination. (NC: KS1 1b)
- Explore how to choose and apply skills and actions in sequence. (NC: KS1 2a)
- Choose and link skills and actions in short phrases. (NC: KS1 8c)
- Create and perform short linked sequences that show a beginning, middle and end and have contrasts in direction, level and speed. (NC: KS1 8d)

English

- Use wide-ranging vocabulary. (NC: KS1 En3 1a)
- Attempt to write unfamiliar words. (NC: KS1 En3 2a)
- Form letters of a regular size and shape. (NC: KS1 En3 5d)

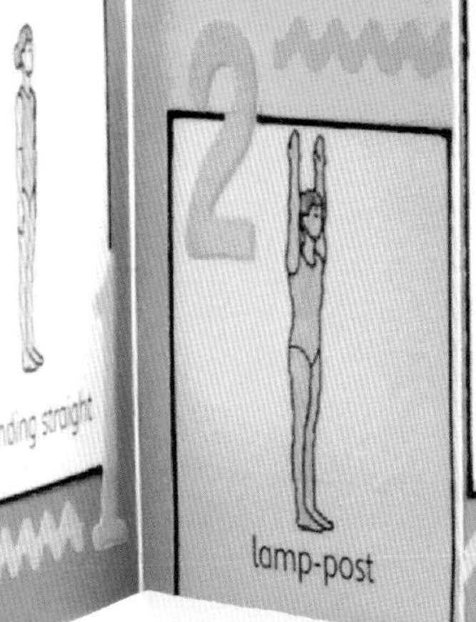

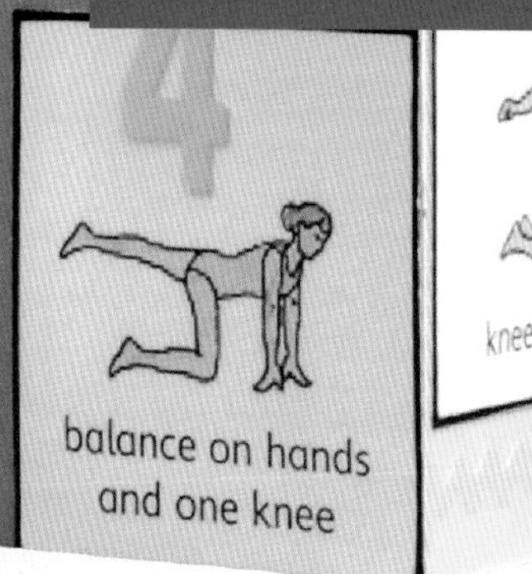

Lesson 2 **Invent a game**

AGES 7–9

Objectives
- To play a simple game and suggest how to improve it.
- To invent a team game.
- To play in a team.

Subject references
Physical education
- Play and make up small-sided and modified competitive net, striking/fielding and invasion games. (NC: KS2 7b)
- Use skills and tactics and apply basic principles suitable for attacking and defending.
- Work with others to organise and keep games going. (NC: KS2 7c)
- Make contributions relevant to the topic and take turns in discussion.

English
(NC: KS2 En1 3a)
- Vary contributions to suit the activity and purpose, including exploratory and tentative comments, where ideas are being collected together and reasoned, evaluative comments as discussion moves to conclusions or action. (NC: KS2 En1 3b)
- Deal politely with opposing points of view and enable discussion to move on. (NC: KS2 En1 3d)

Resources and preparation
Each pair of children will need: a copy of photocopiable page 62, a cup and dice, a counter or small card circle, which could be drawn on to make it look like a football. The children will need to use the school hall or gym to try out their games.

Starter
- Talk about some of the indoor sports that take place in the modern Olympics and talk about how some sports are newly introduced while others are dropped – see the Background information on page 56. Focus on some of the team games that are played.
- Tell the children that they are going to look at team games, starting with a simple board game that has been made up for them to try.
- Give out the copies of photocopiable page 62, the cup, dice and 'football'. Go through the rules with the children, given at the bottom of the photocopiable sheet, then let them try the game.

What to do
- Now tell the children that you want them to invent a new team sport for the Olympics. They will be able to try this game in the gym or school hall. Specify that the game can involve any number of players and a ball. The ball can be kicked or it can be thrown, but not both.
- Advise the children that when making the rules they should consider points such as whether a kick or throw-on goal may or may not be allowed from a player's own half. If the players are to aim for a goal that is a space between two cones, the width of the cones must be set before play. They may also like to add more unusual rules, such as making the cones narrower or wider, once a team has scored.
- Let the children work in pairs or larger groups. They should produce a layout for the pitch, specify the number of players in the team, and consider rules for the goalkeepers, defenders and attackers. All the rules should be written down carefully.
- Examine the games that are produced and select one or more to be tried out with supervision, in the hall or gym.
- Remind the children about the importance of warming up and cooling down before and after playing the game.
- After each game has been tried, the members of both teams must write down or discuss what they thought about the game. Children who have been spectators should also write down their views or air them in a discussion.

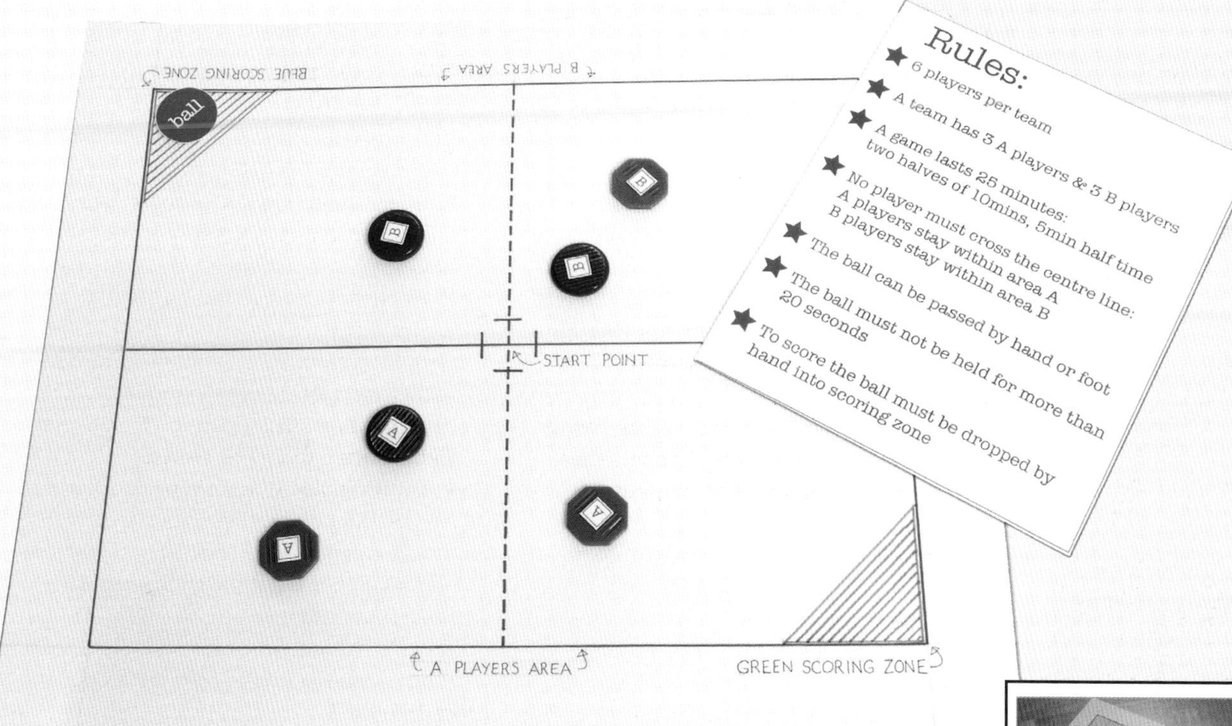

PHOTOGRAPH © PETER ROWE

Differentiation

- Less confident learners may need help in concentrating on the rules in the starter game. They may need prompting to take part in discussions and reminding about the warming up and cooling down activities they have learned previously.
- More confident learners could extend the rules to the board game, such as setting a time limit for the game; deciding that the goalkeeper cannot score; making another set of choices, for example 1–3 score, 4–6 miss.

ILLUSTRATION © LASZLO VERES/BEEHIVE ILLUSTRATION

Assessment

The children can be assessed on their ideas to invent a game or their contribution to the team they are working in, such as taking the lead and organising a discussion or writing down the rules as the children debate them. They could be assessed on how well they played in the team game.

Plenary

The most popular game could be made into a knock-out tournament in which four teams take part. The teams draw lots for who they play in the first round, then the winners of the first round games play for first and second place and the losers of the first round play for third and fourth place.

Outcomes

- The children can play a board game, evaluate it and improve it.
- They can invent a team game which can be played safely.
- They can work in a discussion group and play in a team.

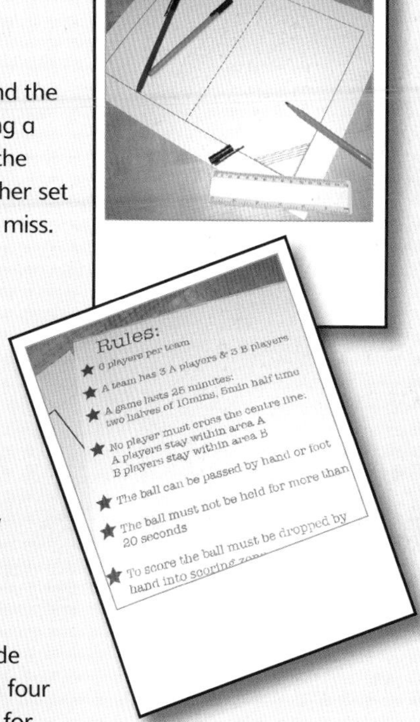

Lesson 3 Which indoor sports?

AGES 9–11

Objectives

- To know about the indoor sports that take place at the Olympic Games
- To reflect on personal sporting traits and match sporting traits to sporting requirements.
- To practise a sporting skill.

Subject references

English

- Make contributions relevant to a topic and take turns in discussion. (NC: KS2 En1 3a)

Physical education

- Consolidate their existing skills and gain new ones. (NC: KS2 1a)
- Perform actions and skills with more consistent control and quality. (NC: KS2 1b)

PSHE and citizenship

- Recognise their worth as individuals by identifying positive things about themselves. (NC: KS2 5b)
- Realise that their actions affect others, care about others' feelings and see their points of view. (NC: KS2 4a)

Resources and preparation

- Each child will need a copy of photocopiable page 63. You will also need: netballs, basketballs and the hoops.
- You may like to reshape this lesson using the first part of Theme 6, Lesson 3, having half the class considering outdoor sports and the other half considering indoor sports. A second lesson would combine the extensions to these lessons.

What to do

- Begin by asking the children to stick up their thumbs. See them discover that some thumbs stick straight up, and some bend backwards. Lead into the concept that everyone has different characteristics, some of which are useful in sport.
- Give out photocopiable page 63 and read the first section with the children. Let the children write down their thoughts on their sporting characteristics and discuss them with their friends. Be prepared for heated discussion! Stress that it is natural and positive for everyone to be different.
- Move on to a class discussion of each sport, considering personal traits that may be suitable for success. Some children may already take part in a sport they can talk about.
- Let the children select sports to which they may be suited. Emphasise that if someone really likes a sport they can work on any weaknesses to make themselves successful competitors.
- Note that some of the sports are inappropriate for children as their bodies are still growing fast, and that some combat sports are only suitable for adults.

Extension

- Encourage existing competitors to give a presentation about their sport.
- The children could look at an Olympics website and browse the photographs for three sports they would like to try. They could print these and attach them to their copy of photocopiable page 63 (copyright permitting).
- Remind the children that practising a skill improves competence and let them take turns at shooting in netball and basketball. If nets and baskets are not available, let them practise throwing to each other and catching over increasing distances.

Did you know?

A table tennis ball can travel at 160 km per hour, when hit on the volley.

Gymnastics

standing straight	 lamp-post	 dish	 walking forward
 walking backward	 skip	 hop	 jog
 crocodile	 bunny jump	 egg roll	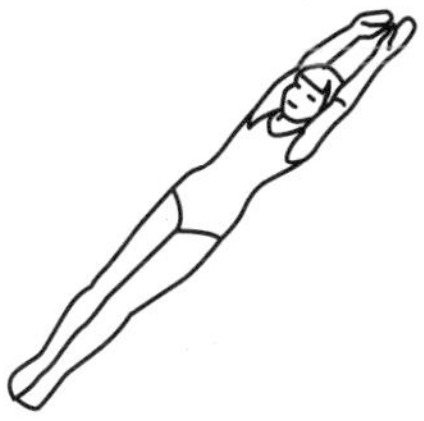 pencil roll
 one-leg balance	 knee balance	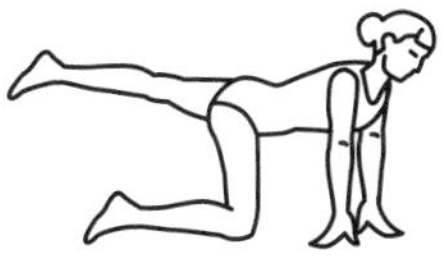 balance on hands and one knee	 jump
 thin-shape jump	 wide-shape jump		

Invent a game

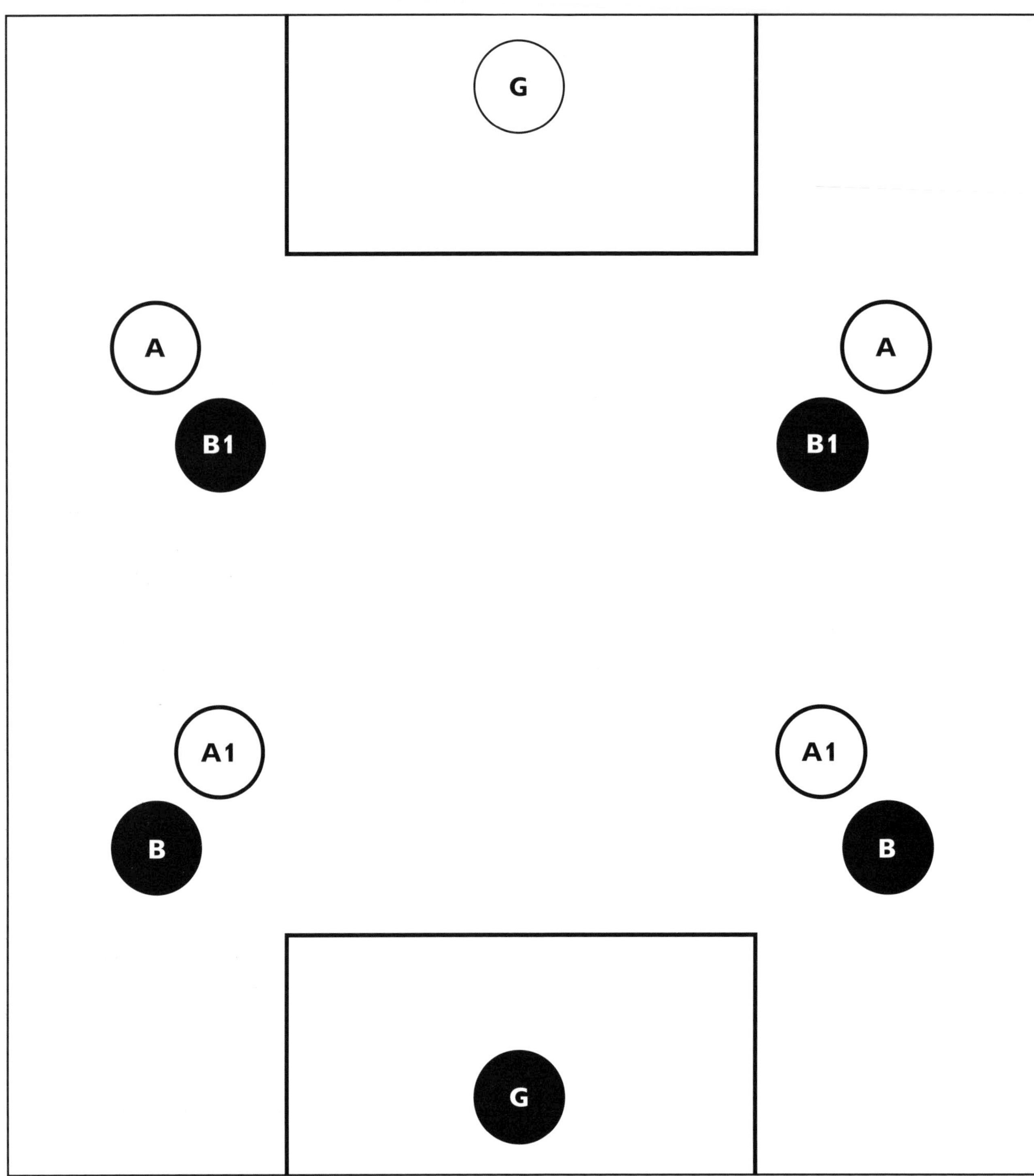

Throw:
1 – Pass across
2 – Pass back
3 – Pass forward
4 – Pass to nearest opponent
5 – Pass diagonally to opponent in other half of pitch
6 – Score

Which indoor sports?

Everyone has skills or qualities. Here are some needed for certain sports:

- Strength
- Flexibility
- Stamina
- Fast-moving
- Quick reactions
- Good sense of balance
- Keen vision (able to see small objects at a distance).

Which do you have?

Here are the indoor Olympic sports. What traits would each champion need? Which three sports might you be good at in the future?

Diving: High and low dives with twists and somersaults.

Swimming: Freestyle (crawl), breast stroke, back stroke, butter fly, relay.

Synchronised swimming: Make ballet moves, hold breath underwater, move to music.

Water polo: Two teams of seven, swim and throw and catch a ball and shoot it at a goal.

Badminton: Use a racket to hit a shuttlecock over a high net, run and jump.

Basketball: Two teams of five run, jump and throw, catch, bounce a ball and shoot into a basket 3m high.

Boxing: Strike an opponent with gloved hands and move to evade blows.

Fencing: Move quickly backwards and forwards striking an opponent with tip or side of the sword.

Gymnastics: Run, jump, roll, balance, hang from bars or hoops and somersault.

Handball: Two teams of seven run, throw, catch and bounce a ball and score goals.

Judo: Throw or wrestle an opponent to the ground, and hold them there.

Table tennis: Move quickly and use a small bat to strike a ball over a low net.

Taekwondo: Kick and punch an opponent while twisting and spinning.

Volleyball: Two teams of six jump and use hands to get a large ball over a high net.

Weightlifting: Lift heavy weights on a steel rod, requiring many different muscles.

Wrestling: Throw an opponent or hold them on the ground so that they cannot move.

Theme 8

Olympics worldwide

BACKGROUND

Lessons 1 and 2 continue looking at the summer games. The information here supports Lesson 3, which features the Winter Olympics and the Paralympics.

Winter Olympics are held every four years – two years after a summer games. Ice skating was first introduced in the 1908 London (summer) Olympics and became an official winter Olympic sport in 1924. Ice hockey was introduced in 1920. Fewer athletes take part in the Winter Olympics as many countries do not have the climate or facilities to practise for competition. The events that take place include alpine (downhill) skiing, biathlon (cross country skiing with shooting), bobsleigh, cross country skiing, curling, figure skating, speed skating, ice hockey, luge, ski jumping, snowboarding, skeleton bob.

The work on games for people with disabilities should be handled with sensitivity. Its aim is to show that people need not be excluded from sport because of disability. The Paralympic Games are for athletes with disabilities such as lost limbs, spinal injuries, poor sight and cerebral palsy. These games were established in 1960 and now take place three weeks after the main summer games, at the same venue. Sports include archery, athletics, cycling, fencing, horse riding, judo, swimming, table tennis.

There are also games for the hearing impaired – the Deaflympics (summer and winter games since 1924), and the Special Olympics World Games for people with learning difficulties (summer and winter).

THE CONTENTS

Lesson 1 (Ages 5–7)
Olympics timeline

The children arrange the dates and venues in a timeline. They look at the venues around the globe.

Lesson 2 (Ages 7–9)
Olympic venues

The children make a timeline of Olympic venues and use a world map or atlas to locate 16 of them. They also look at an Olympic village.

Lesson 3 (Ages 9–11)
Olympics for all

The children survey the summer Olympic venues before moving on to the winter venues. They consider sports for people with disabilities.

Notes on photocopiables
Olympics timeline (page 69)

Note that there is a blank box for the venue in 2016.The order is: Athens 1896, Paris 1900, St Louis 1904, London 1908, Stockholm 1912, Antwerp 1920, Paris 1924, Amsterdam 1928, Los Angeles 1932, Berlin 1936, London 1948, Helsinki 1952, Melbourne 1956, Rome 1960, Tokyo 1964, Mexico City 1968, Munich 1972, Montreal 1976, Moscow 1980, Los Angeles 1984, Seoul 1988, Barcelona 1992, Atlanta 1996, Sydney 2000, Athens 2004, Beijing 2008, London 2012.

Olympic venues (page 70)

16 venues are labelled A–P: A) Los Angeles, B) Mexico City, C) St Louis, D) Montreal, E) London, F) Paris, G) Berlin, H) Stockholm, I) Helsinki, J) Moscow, K) Rome, L) Athens, M) Beijing, N) Tokyo, O) Melbourne, P) Sydney. Six venues are not labelled, for more confident children to find using an atlas index: Atlanta, Barcelona, Antwerp, Amsterdam, Munich, Seoul.

Olympics for all (page 71)

This map shows some winter Olympic venues: A) Salt Lake City, B) Calgary, C) Lake Placid, D) Chamonix, E) St Moritz, F) Oslo, G) Lillehammer, H) Innsbruck, I) Sarajevo, J) Nagano, K) Sappora, L) Vancouver.

Lesson 1 Olympics timeline

AGES 5–7

Objectives
- To appreciate that the modern Olympics have been taking place for a long time.
- To know that the modern Olympics are held at different places around the world.

Subject references
History
- Place events in chronological order. (NC: KS1 1a)
- Identify different ways in which the past is represented. (NC: KS1 3)
- Learn about past events in from the history of Britain and the wider world. (NC: KS1 6d)

Mathematics
- Read numbers beyond 100. (NC: KS1 Ma2 2c)

Geography
- Use globes and maps. (NC: KS1 2c)

Resources and preparation
- Each child will need: a copy of photocopiable page 69, scissors, glue and a strip of paper 5cm wide and 120cm long. The class will need a globe or large map of the world.
- You may also like to prepare a long line of years (1896, 1897, 1898, 1899, 1900 and so on, into the 21st century) to attach the names of venues to for an accurate timeline.

What to do
- Remind the children about how the ancient Olympic Games ended and the new one began (see pages 40 and 47 in Theme 5). Go on to say that, unlike the ancient Olympics (which was always held in Olympia) the modern games, has been held all, over the world.
- Give out copies of photocopiable page 69 and let the children cut out the boxes and arrange them in chronological order.
- When you have checked the order made by each child let the children stick their boxes, side by side, onto the strip of paper to make their timelines.
- Show the children the date line you have prepared and ask them to call out the names of the venues, in order, so that you can stick the venues on it.
- When you have finished, ask the children to compare their timelines with yours and look for the observation that there are gaps in your timeline. Tell the children that these were due to the games not being held during the two world wars of the 20th century.

Extension
- Show the children a globe or map of the world and ask them to call out the names of the venues, in order, starting in 1896. Show the children the position of each venue in turn.
- Tell the children that an athlete is usually able to take part in more than one Olympic Games. Ask them to pick any three games to show where an athlete might travel to in order to compete.
- Show the children how far they would have to travel from the UK, to visit the next Olympic Games.

Lesson 2 Olympic venues

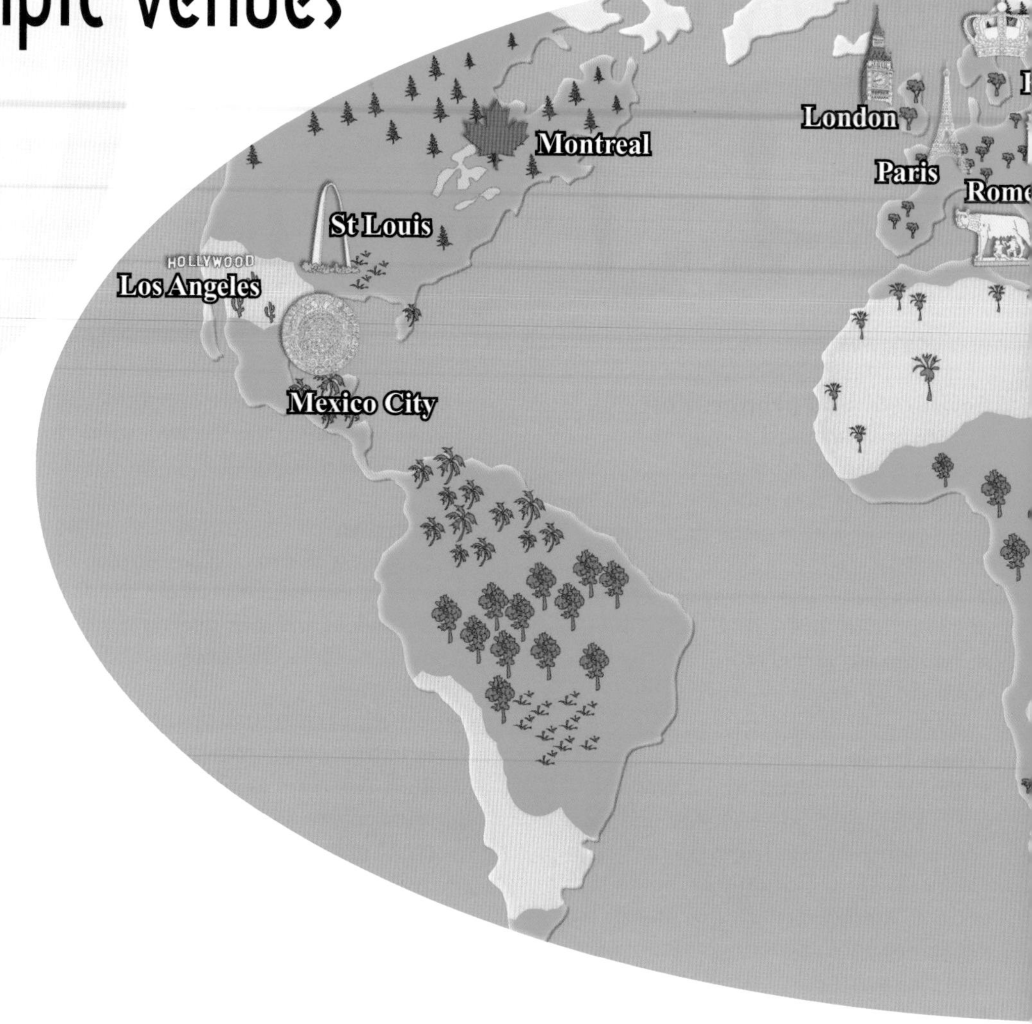

AGES 7–9

Objectives
- To place modern Olympic Games in chronological order.
- To find and identify places on a map.
- To produce a map showing some of the venues of the modern Olympic Games.

Subject references

History
- Place events into correct periods of time. (NC: KS2 1a)
- Find out about events from an appropriate source. (NC: KS2 4a)
- Select and organise historical information. (NC: KS2 5a)
- Communicate their knowledge of history in a variety of ways. (NC: KS2 5c)

Geography
- Use maps. (NC: KS2 2c)
- Locate places they study. (NC: KS2 3b)
- Study a range of places in different parts of the world. (NC: KS2 7b)

Resources and preparation
- Each child or pair of children will need: copies of photocopiable pages 69 and 70, scissors, glue, rulers, a world map or atlas which features major cities, a larger sheet of card on which the map from page 70 can be mounted and which provides space to stick on the boxes of the venues from page 69. More confident learners may need more detailed atlases with indexes.
- You will need classroom assistance to help less confident learners work with the maps. For the Plenary, you could refer to relevant websites for the 2012 Olympics.
- You may also like to prepare a long line of years (1896, 1897, 1898, 1899, 1900... into the 21st century) to attach the names of venues to for an accurate timeline.

Starter
- Tell the children that since 1896, the modern Olympic Games have been held in many different cities all over the world.
- Give out copies of photocopiable page 69 and let the children cut out the boxes and arrange them in chronological order side by side, starting with Athens 1896 on the left.
- Show the children the date line you have prepared and ask them to call out the names of the venues in order, so that you can stick the venue boxes on it. When you have finished, ask the children to compare their timelines with yours and see if they notice that the gaps in your timeline.

Tell or elicit from the children that these were due to the games not being held during the two world wars of the 20th century.

What to do
- Tell the children to collect up the venue boxes from their timelines.
- Give out copies of photocopiable page 70 and maps or atlases and ask the children to identify the venues labelled A to P. Check their answers with the information given on page 64.
- Issue the large cards and ask the children to stick their maps in the middle of them.

ILLUSTRATION © LASZLO VERES/BEEHIVE ILLUSTRATION

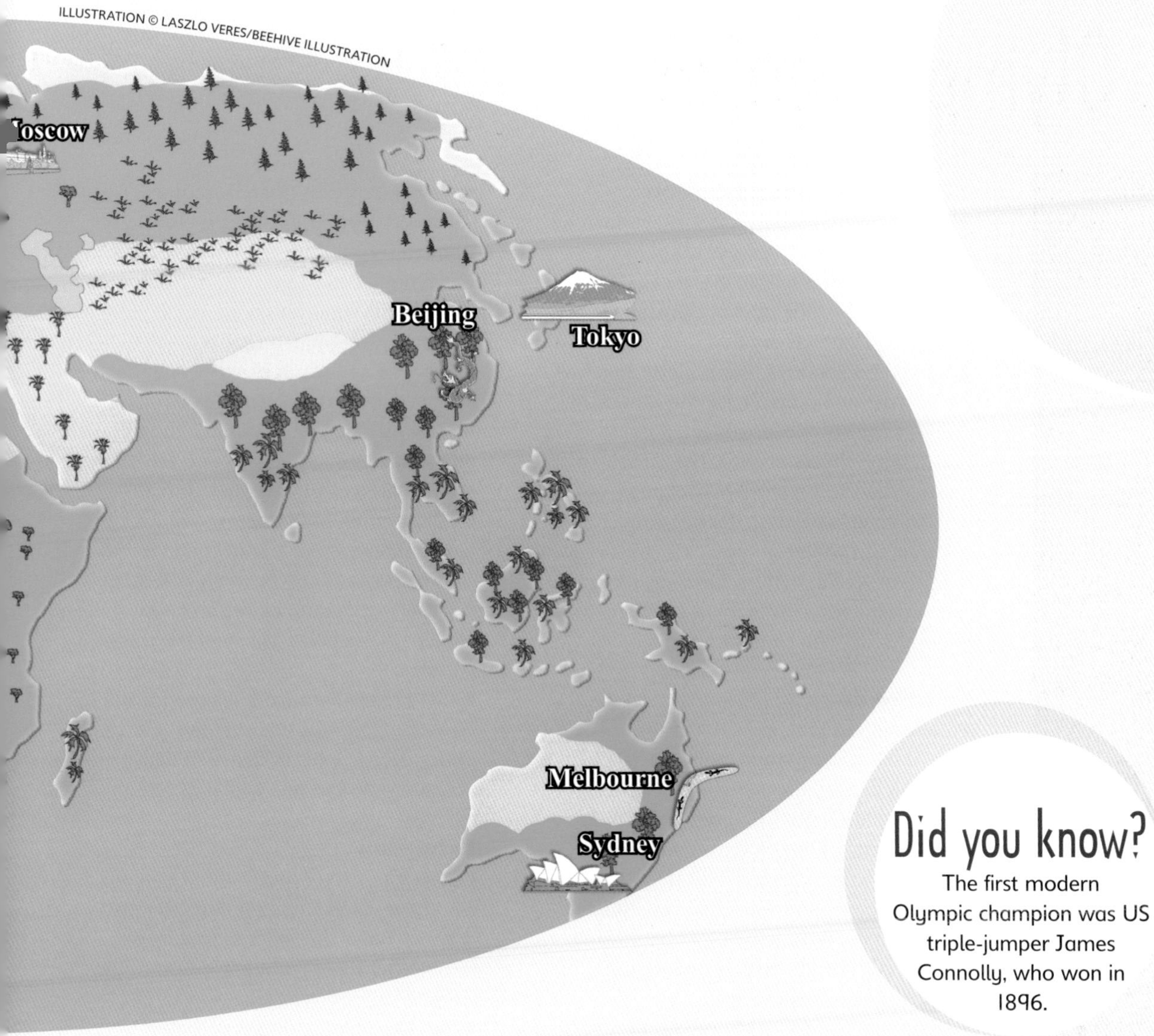

Did you know?

The first modern Olympic champion was US triple-jumper James Connolly, who won in 1896.

- Ask the children to begin labelling the map by sticking the venue box for Los Angeles in the left margin and drawing a line from the box to dot A.
- Let the children work on matching each venue box to its city dot, sticking the box down and drawing a label line. For clarity, they should make sure that the label lines do not cross each other. Ensure the children understand that not all the venues listed have been highlighted on the map.
- The maps could then be made into a wall display.

Differentiation

- Less confident learners will need help in making their timelines. They may also need help identifying the venues on the map.
- More confident learners could use more detailed atlases with indexes, to locate the venues Atlanta, Barcelona, Antwerp, Amsterdam, Munich and Seoul. They could then add these labels (from photocopiable page 69) to their maps.

Assessment

Assess the children on the ease with which they constructed their timelines, the accuracy in locating venues and the presentation of their labelled maps.

Plenary

- Discuss with the children that a great deal of time, organisation and expense is involved in providing a venue for the Olympics. Along with indoor and outdoor stadiums, in which the athletes can compete, there also needs to be accommodation for the athletes and the officials to live in, during the games. An Olympic village is built to provide everything that is needed.
- Describe an Olympic village; you may want to refer to the 2012 Olympics web page from BBC News.

Outcomes

- The children can arrange Olympic venues in chronological order.
- They can use maps to locate many of the venues.
- They can label a map of the world with Olympic venues.

Lesson 3 Olympics for all

AGES 9–11

Objectives
- To find on a map and identify venues of the summer and winter Olympic Games.
- To learn about the games for people with disabilities.

Subject references
Geography
- Use maps. (NC: KS2 2c)
- Locate places they study. (NC: KS2 3b)

History
- Find out about events from a range of sources. (NC: KS2 4a)

ICT
- Work with a range of information to consider its characteristics and purposes. (NC: KS2 5a)

PSHE and citizenship
- Recognise and challenge stereotypes. (NC: KS2 4e)

Resources and preparation
- If the children have previously completed photocopiable page 15, ask them to produce it for this lesson. Read Lesson 2, page 66, as the first part of this lesson adapts and extends on it.
- Photocopy pages 69 and 70 for one half of the class and page 71 for the other. The children will also need: atlases, scissors, glue, rulers, large sheets of card. There are useful photographs to view at www.olympic.org/uk/games/index_uk.asp. (Scroll down to summer and winter games, click on a venue, then scroll to the bottom for the gallery.) The website www.paralympic.org can be referred to for the Extension.

What to do
- Referring to photocopiable page 15, remind the children that athletes travelled to Olympia from all over Ancient Greece. Tell the children that they are going to look at this aspect of the modern games too.
- Explain to the children that there are summer games and winter games, and issue photocopiable pages 69 and 70. Tell them to cut out the venues on page 69 and arrange them chronologically.
- Then ask them to stick the map from page 70 in the centre of the large card and use an atlas to identify the venues. They should then stick the venue labels around the map and add label lines.
- Give out copies of photocopiable page 71 and challenge the children to use an atlas to identify the venues. Give them two examples – Lake Placid (C) and Chamonix (D). Explain that not all the venues listed are shown on the map, as the map scale is too small. The country is given to help children select an area to search.
- Ask the children to make a map display as for the summer venues and see all the different places athletes travel to.
- Draw attention to winter venues being in places where there is snow and ice, but that summer venues can be in any climate.
- Look at the date cycles and elicit that the winter games occur between the summer games.
- Let the children work independently to view the Olympics website and select and print photographic evidence of activities at one summer and one winter games.

Extension
- Introduce the concept that people who have disabilities can also take part in sport. Refer the children to quiz on the International Paralympic Committee website.
- Let the children access the site themselves and visit the Profile/Athlete of the month. They could then survey the athletes and list the sports at which they excel.

Olympics timeline

Athens 1896	St Louis 1904	Paris 1900	Los Angeles 1932
Amsterdam 1928	London 1908	Stockholm 1912	Los Angeles 1984
London 2012	Antwerp 1920	Athens 2004	Paris 1924
Berlin 1936	Seoul 1988	London 1948	Montreal 1976
Barcelona 1992	Helsinki 1952	Melbourne 1956	Beijing 2008
Rome 1960	Munich 1972	Sydney 2000	Tokyo 1964
Mexico City 1968	Atlanta 1996	Moscow 1980	

Olympic venues

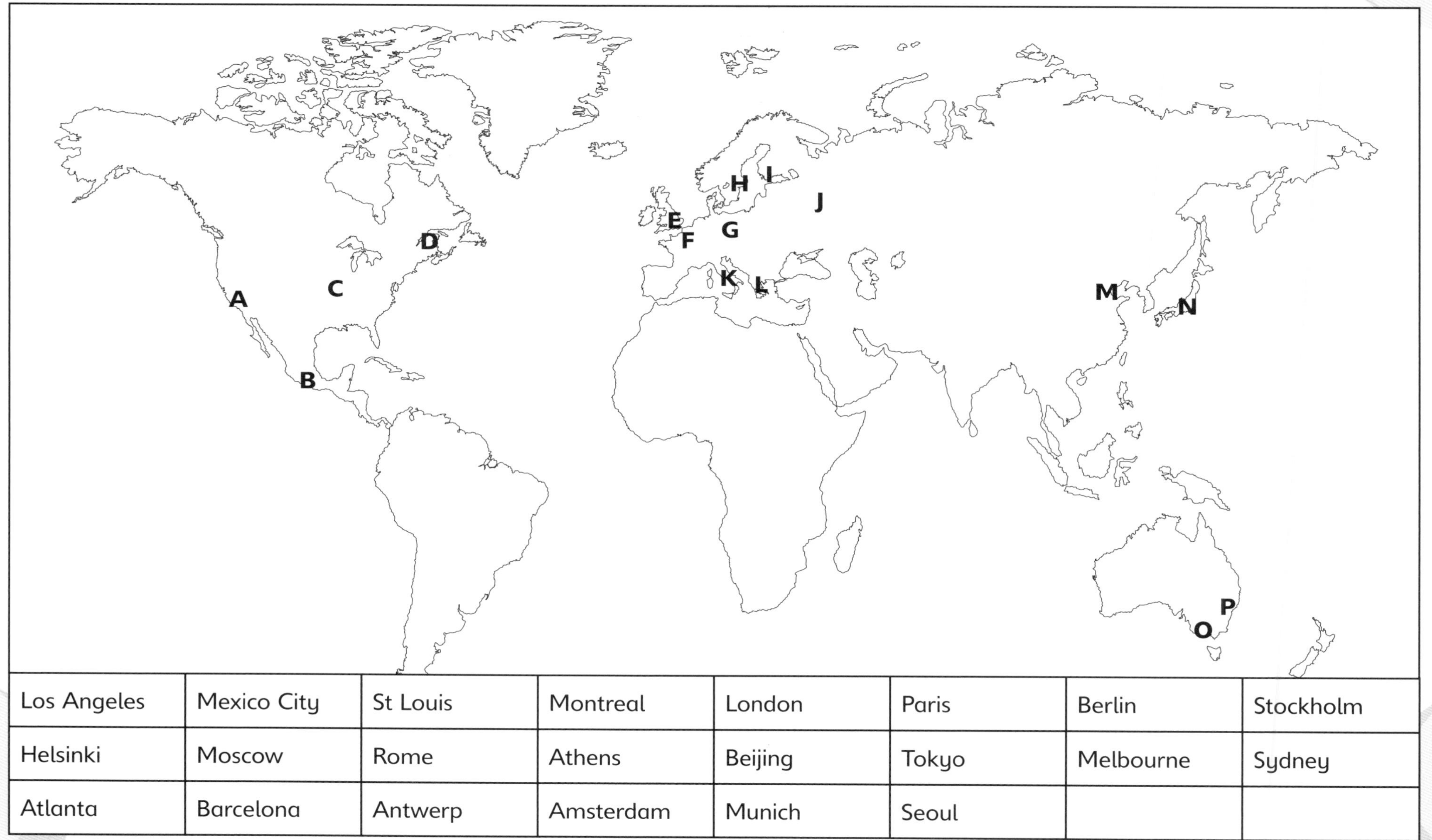

Los Angeles	Mexico City	St Louis	Montreal	London	Paris	Berlin	Stockholm
Helsinki	Moscow	Rome	Athens	Beijing	Tokyo	Melbourne	Sydney
Atlanta	Barcelona	Antwerp	Amsterdam	Munich	Seoul		

Olympics for all

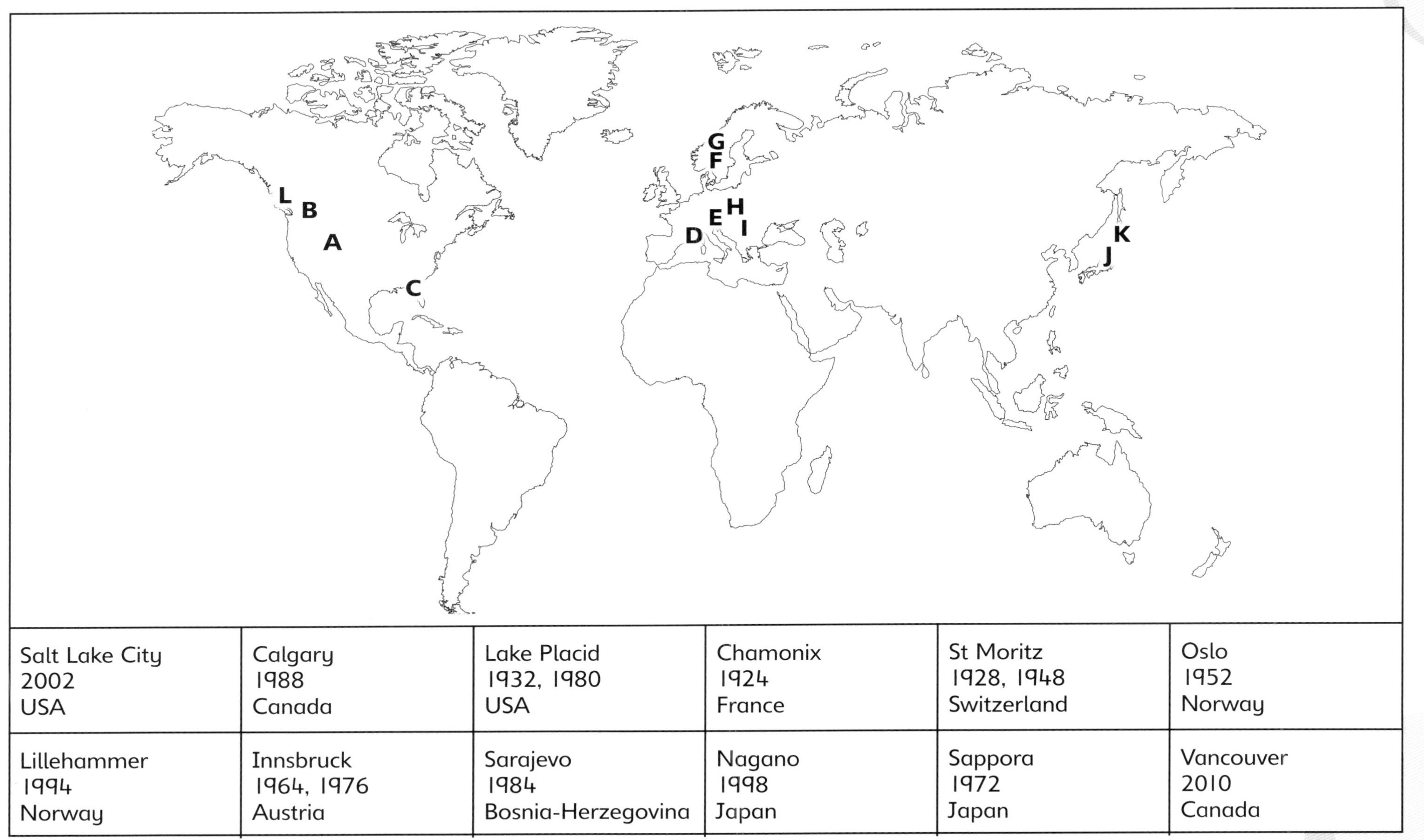

Salt Lake City 2002 USA	Calgary 1988 Canada	Lake Placid 1932, 1980 USA	Chamonix 1924 France	St Moritz 1928, 1948 Switzerland	Oslo 1952 Norway
Lillehammer 1994 Norway	Innsbruck 1964, 1976 Austria	Sarajevo 1984 Bosnia-Herzegovina	Nagano 1998 Japan	Sappora 1972 Japan	Vancouver 2010 Canada

Theme 9

Champions

BACKGROUND

The spectacular opening and closing ceremonies of the Olympic Games have links with the ancient games. The Olympic flame, which represents the death and rebirth of Greek heroes, was originally used to light the fire at an altar and today, it is lit and transported to the venue by relay as described on page 48. At the venue, a huge cauldron is lit by the torch and it stays alight for the duration of the games.

There were music contests in the ancient games, and music continues to be a feature of Olympic ceremonies. Doves, which symbolise peace, are released during the opening ceremony. The winner's olive branch appears as a symbol on today's medals. A statue of Nike, the goddess of victory, accompanied the statue of Zeus in his temple and today, she is also found on medals. The Olympic gold medal is made of sterling silver coated in gold. A medal called the Pierre de Coubertin medal is given, only rarely, to an athlete who displays great sportsmanship. The Olympic movement has an oath and a motto: *Citius, altius, fortius* which means *Swifter, higher, stronger.*

People's natural physical features and abilities help them to become successful at sports, but factors such as upbringing, training, coaching and psychological talents such as coping with pressure in competitions, are also believed to contribute.

THE CONTENTS

Lesson 1 Ages (5–7)
Old Olympics, new Olympics

The children learn a song about the Olympics. The music is written for piano. The fanfare consists of two bars repeated as necessary and should go straight into the song. The right hand plays the melody which the children sing and the left hand has simple chordal accompaniment which emphasises the marching beat. Other instruments are not needed as the children will be singing and parading. Some verses are wordier than others, and the hyphens show where the syllables fall. The children may like to perform with use of mime and gymnastics.

Lesson 2 (Ages 7–9)
Mascots and medals

The children design a mascot and medals for the school Olympic Games.

Lesson 3 (Ages 9–11)
A good competitor

The children read and respond to questions in a sports interview. They consider other questions they would like to ask a visiting sports star and draw up an interview sheet.

Notes on photocopiables
Olympic song (page 77)

This song is about the old Olympics and the attributes of champions and the medals they can win.

Mascots and medals (page 78)

The two circles form the front and back of a medal. Olympic symbols can be cut out and stuck on the sides of the medal. There are spaces for children to draw their own symbols.

A good competitor (page 79)

This series of questions could be put to a successful competitor. There are spaces for the children to respond. The sheet can form the basis of a fuller interview script.

Lesson 1 Old Olympics, new Olympics

Resources and preparation
- Each child or group will need a photocopy of page 77.
- You may want the children to perform in costume (see the project-planning notes on page 7). The children could begin in Ancient Greek clothing, and those coming on towards the end of the performance could be in modern athletic clothes.

What to do
- Tell the children that they are going to learn a song about the Olympics. As you go through the words on the sheet, remind the children about their previous studies. They should know that a truce was called throughout Ancient Greece when the games were held, and about the sporting events that took place at Olympia. They should also know the fate of Olympia and that today's athletes win gold, silver and bronze medals.
- Teach the song and rehearse it for a performance.

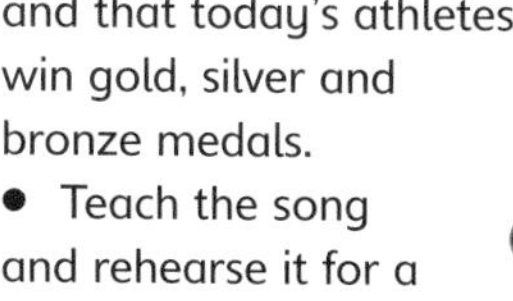

Extension
The song can be developed into a more complex performance, which the children will need to rehearse:
1) The fanfare can be used as the choir walks onto the stage, or repeated as the whole school forms a parade. When the procession stops in front of the audience, the choir sings the first line, during which two heralds come centre stage and then move to stand at each side.
2) In Verse 2, some of the children could mime the actions as they are sung.
3) In Verse 3, all the children tremble when singing the first line. In the second line, some of them can fall down. In the third line, the choir can point to the side of the stage from where more children dressed in modern athletic clothes can come on and perform simple gymnastic moves.
4) In the final verse, all the children sing. In line 3, three more children come on wearing a gold, silver or bronze medal which they hold up. Three more children can come on during the last line to give flowers to the medallists. At the end of the song, everyone gives three cheers.

AGES 5–7

Objectives
- To learn and perform a song.
- To devise and perform actions to accompany the song.

Subject references
Music
- Use voices expressively by singing songs. (NC: KS1 1a)
- Rehearse and perform with others. (NC: KS1 1c)
- Express their feelings about music using movement. (NC: KS1 3a)
- Work as a class. (NC: KS1 5c)

Physical education
- Use movement imaginatively, responding to stimuli, including music, and performing basic skills. (NC: KS1 6a)

Lesson 2 Mascots and medals

AGES 7–9

Objectives
- To learn that each Olympic games has a mascot.
- To design a school's Olympic mascot purse.
- To learn about the features of an Olympic medal and construct one.

Subject references
Art and design
- Collect visual and other information to help develop ideas. (NC: KS2 1c)

Design and technology
- Develop ideas and explain them clearly, putting together a list of what they want their design to achieve. (NC: KS2 1b)
- Select appropriate tools and techniques for making their product. (NC: KS2 2a)
- Measure and mark out, cut and shape a range of materials and assemble join and combine components and materials accurately. (NC: KS2 2d)

Resources and preparation
- For the mascot purses, the children will need: a selection of fabrics and fastenings, scissors, fabric glue, needles and threads, fabric colouring pencils and paints. For the medals, they will need: photocopiable page 78 copied onto yellow/gold card, scissors, glue, sticky tape, shiny gold paper, a length of blue ribbon long enough to make a loop so the medal hangs at stomach height. More confident children may want photocopiable page 23.
- For examples of Olympic mascots and medals, visit www.olympic.org/uk/passion/collectors/search_uk.asp?TypeId=4.

Starter
- Tell the children that since 1968 winter and summer Olympic Games have had mascots. Suggest that it would be good to have a mascot for their school Olympic Games on Olympics Day. Can the children design one? Show them some examples from the website, on an interactive whiteboard. Click on the mascots from different years. You could let the children indicate whether they particularly like a mascot by raising their hands as you click on each one. Alternatively you could go through them all and then let the children discuss what they have seen.
- Point out that the mascot has something to do with the host country – for example an animal that is found there and is associated with the country – and suggest to the children that their mascot should have something to do with the school or the local area.
- Let the children decide on a mascot and then tell them that they are to make a purse, which either has the shape of the mascot or features a picture of it. Let the children begin their designs, including a plan of how to make the purse, ready for reflection and construction in another lesson.

What to do
- Remind the children that in the ancient Olympics, the winner of an event was crowned with an olive branch bent into a circle. It was called a *kotinos*. Today, winners receive medals – gold, silver and bronze for first, second and third places.
- Give out the card copies of photocopiable page 78 and tell the children that they are going to make a gold medal to wear at some time on Olympics Day (even if they do not win an event).
- Point out the traditional Olympic emblems – the torch, the dove of peace, the small and large *kotinos* and small and large figures of Nike, the goddess of victory. There

PHOTOGRAPHS © PETER ROWE

are also two borders which can be used for the children's emblems.

- Return to the website you used for mascots and point out the main Olympic emblem of five interlocking rings, signifying the five continents where Olympic athletes come from.
- While you are on the website, view some of the medal designs from previous summer Olympics.
- Tell the children that they are going to design their own medal. Explain that they can use any of the emblems and designs on the card and use the two spaces to draw their own ideas for emblems which represent the school or the area.
- Let the children work to cover the medal in gold paper and cut out and stick the emblems into place. They should finish by using sticky paper to attach a length of blue ribbon to the medal in a loop.

Differentiation

- Less dextrous learners may need help in cutting out the plain or studded border and the large *kotinos*. Less confident learners may need help in thinking about using emblems, which represent the school or the area.
- More confident learners could use the Greek alphabet on photocopiable page 23 to help them write a short message or the school's name on the medal.

Assessment

The children can be assessed on the quality of the presentation of the medal, and their designs for school emblems.

Plenary

Let the children hang up their medals for display. When the purses are finished, they can be placed on a table below the medals for display.

Outcomes

- The children learn about Olympic mascots and design their own.
- They make their own gold medals. Olympic emblems.

Lesson 3 A good competitor

AGES 9–11

Objectives

- To consider factors that make someone a good competitor.
- To ask questions politely.

Subject references

English

- Speak audibly and clearly, using spoken standard English in formal contexts. (NC: KS2 En1 1e)
- Identify the gist of an account and evaluate what they hear. (NC: KS2 2a)
- Ask relevant questions to clarify, extend or follow up ideas. (NC: KS2 En1 2b)
- Recall and re-present important features of a talk. (NC: KS2 2c)
- Listen to live talks. (NC: KS2 9a)
- Sustain different roles, individually. (NC: KS2 En1 4a)
- Use dramatic techniques to explore issues. (NC: KS2 En1 4c)

PHOTOGRAPH © GETTY IMAGES/STU FORSTER

Resources and preparation

- If you are planning to hold an interview (see Extension), your chosen sports figure should be contacted well in advance, and a copy of photocopiable page 79 should be sent to them with the letter of enquiry to give an idea of the visit's format. Later, a copy of the class interview could be sent for approval.
- Each child will need a copy of photocopiable page 79. Before the Extension, a new and longer interview sheet can be prepared. You could keep a master copy and use it to organise the order of questions and who will ask each one. A second copy could be cut up and distributed among the children. A room in a quiet part of the school will be needed for the visit.

What to do

- If you have successfully approached a visitor, tell the children about the visit and introduce the idea that they are going to hold an interview to find out how someone became successful in their sport.
- Give out the photocopies of page 79 and help the children to read through the questions.
- Ask the children to imagine that they are a successful sports star. Prompt them to recall the training they have done for Olympics Day and ask them to answer as many of the questions as they can.
- Discuss their various answers and then ask the children if they have any other questions they would like to ask the visitor. Select questions that you consider appropriate and add them into the list.

Extension

- Distribute the questions for the interview as allocated on your master copy.
- Welcome and introduce the visitor – it could be someone who plays for a local team or who trains at a local athletic club and competes at county or national level. Explain to him or her how the questions will be asked, then start the interview.
- During the interview, the children should try to remember the answer to their question, but you may find it useful to make notes on the master copy.
- At the end of the interview, ask the visitor if he or she would like to add anything. You may also like to allow some time for the children to ask any questions they have thought of during the interview.
- Afterwards, one or more children could give a vote of thanks. If appropriate, invite the visitor to Olympics Day to award the prizes.

Olympic song

Verse 1
Long ago in Ancient Greece,
Heralds called for wars to cease.
People walked and sailed in peace
To take part in the games.

Verse 2
Discus, javelin and jumping,
Boxing, wrestling and running,
Horses, chariots and singing,
At the old Olympic Games

Verse 3
Earthquakes made Olympia crumble,
Statues topple, temples tumble.
In the end we should not grumble,
There are still Olympic Games.

Verse 4
Athletes must be brave and bold,
If they are to win and hold,
Medals bronze, silver and gold,
At the new Olympic Games.

Music by Sally-Anne Riley, Words by Peter Riley

Mascots and medals

A good competitor

1) Which sports did you play when you were about five or six?	2) Which sports were you good at and which were you not very good at?
3) Were any other people in your family good at sports?	4) When did you start taking part in competitions?
5) What was your training schedule when you started to compete?	6) What was your training schedule when you were achieving your greatest success?
7) Did you always find training easy?	8) What do you like best about training?
9) What do you like least about training?	10) Do you take care to eat healthily? If so, what foods do you eat?
11) Which foods do you avoid and why?	12) How did coaching help you to improve?
13) How do you prepare on the day of a competition?	14) What do you think about in the few minutes before the event?
) How do you feel when you have rformed well?	16) How do you feel when you have won?
17) When you do not win, how do you motivate yourself to try again?	18) People look very serious when they are competing. Is there a place for a sense of humour in sport? If there is, when is it useful?

SCHOLASTIC

In this series:

ISBN 978-0439-94509-7

ISBN 978-0439-94552-3

ISBN 978-0439-94510-3

ISBN 978-0439-94573-8

To find out more, call: 0845 603 9091
or visit www.scholastic.co.uk